Meyer's
Bakery

Claus Meyer

Meyer's Bakery

Bread and baking in the Nordic Kitchen

MITCHELL
BEAZLEY

CONTENTS

ANY QUESTIONS?

Has your dough not risen or
have you left your starter for
too long? Don't worry! Email us
at info@meyersusa.com where
you can ask any questions.
We have lots of useful
information, inspiring tips and
regular updates on some of the
recipes in this book which we
would love to share.

WANT TO BAKE WITH US?

At www.greatnorthernfood.com
you will find information about
the Great Northern Food Hall,
which is located in New York City,
along with useful information
on the various baking and
cooking courses we offer.

PREFACE

As far back as I can remember I've loved bread. From the age of seven, I would help the local baker in the village of Wetterberg on the southern Danish island of Lolland, before going to school. And my reward was a bag of freshly baked bread. Later, as a student at Copenhagen Business School, I worked in a bakery on the island of Amager, where, unfortunately, I got the sack because I was too slow. The following day, however, I went to see the master baker and I made him an offer he couldn't refuse: I wanted to sublet the bakery after they'd finished for the day. He was surprised, but he agreed. So when I close my eyes and think back, I vividly remember how proud I was, as I biked across the Langebro inner harbour bridge towards a couple of Copenhagen restaurants with a box of freshly baked bread.

LESS YEAST AND MORE HEAT

That was almost 30 years ago, and ever since, baking has been an integral part of my life. When I look back over the many years I've worked with bread, I see some highly remarkable changes in the ways I work with the different types of dough and bread. First of all, I have slowly but surely worked my way up the temperature scale and down the yeast scale. Back then, 30 years ago, I would use 20 grams of yeast with 1 kilogram of flour and bake the bread at 225°C, Gas Mark 7. Then 15 years ago, I'd use 10 grams of yeast with 1 kilogram of flour and bake the bread at 250°C, Gas Mark 9. While today, I use no more than 2 grams of yeast with 1 kilogram of flour and I bake my everyday bread at no lower than 250°C, Gas Mark 9. At the same time, I've increased the amount of fluid I add to my bread, which means that both my wheat dough and my whole-grain dough are quite 'wet' these days. I also let my bread rise for a minimum of 8 hours, and ideally up to 24 hours (well, for some types of dough, even up to 48 hours).

BAKING WITH A STARTER

I have always been fascinated by the method of baking with a starter. The lactic-acid bacteria content gives all types of bread that delicious, sour taste, which complements the characteristic grain aromas so well. Furthermore, when you use a starter, your bread keeps longer. So using the starter actually helps us make better use of raw ingredients, meaning less food ends up in the bin.

Many people believe that using a starter is strange and difficult, and that it takes some kind of molecular gastronomic insight to even try. But the fact of the matter is that it's quite easy to use and very flexible. Even when you leave it to its own devices in the fridge for weeks or even months, it'll forgive you as soon as it senses the warmth of your kitchen. Small helpings of flour and water are all you need to revive it – read more on pages 37–41. And it's easy to make your own starter following the method on pages 44–5. I guarantee it will increase your enjoyment of baking!

USE YOUR SENSES WHEN BAKING BREAD

This book contains the recipes and techniques we have developed over the past 30 years at our food school, Meyer's Madhus in Copenhagen and our bakeries. In 2009, we published *Meyer's Bakery* in Denmark, and in the eight years since then we have continued to develop and refine our methods, particularly for our starter doughs. This constant gathering of knowledge allows us to present you with a very clear method for baking your own bread.

One of the main discoveries we made was that rather than adhering to rigid baking times and temperatures, it's important to trust all of our senses. Of course, we include a guide to timelines and temperatures in all our recipes, but as soon as you get used to smelling, tasting, feeling, listening, and watching what's going on with your dough and your bread, you'll realize that you get much better results. And baking becomes a lot more fun than if you merely set the oven temperature and a timer.

ONE BASIC RECIPE – LOTS OF VARIATIONS

We have structured this book in a way that allows us first to present a thorough introduction to baking equipment and tools. In my opinion, some things are must-haves while others may be considered nice to have and even a little anorakish, yet they most certainly increase the enjoyment of baking. This is followed by advice on using high-quality organic produce, and we take you through the different types of grain and flour we use. Then we tell you everything we know about working with a starter. After which we move on to the four main chapters about wheat bread, whole-grain bread, rye bread, and enriched doughs. Each main chapter takes you through the ingredients, the different methods of mixing, rising, and baking, followed by one or more basic recipes and several variations on these.

We have presented the book this way because it reflects the way we think, work, and develop new types of bread. The feedback from our baking classes has taught us that this is the insight that novice bakers are craving.

Once you gain a more solid understanding of what actually happens along each step of the way, and you understand the different options open to you and how they each affect the finished product, you'll find baking so much easier and your bread will be so much better.

Therefore this is a book for bakers who wish to follow a recipe to ensure a good result, and for those who prefer experimenting and varying recipes depending on what ingredients are to hand and what the day dictates.

QUALITY AND ECOLOGY = BAKING HAPPINESS

Once you've read and understood this book, and after practicing for a while, you'll be able to bake a wonderfully tasty loaf of bread using just about any type of flour. However, both the making and the eating of your bread will be so much more enjoyable if you use high-quality organic flour.

Fortunately for us, there are many producers in Denmark and the other Nordic countries who put a lot of effort into growing high-quality products and who delight in exploring the diversity in grains that prosper in our part of the world. A few years ago, we entered into collaboration with one of this movement's pioneers, Per Grupe, and we support his effort to identify heritage grains such as Øland wheat and *svedjerug* (slash-and-burn) rye that will enrich the food we make from them. We help each other plan the production of the different types of grain at the farms we collaborate with, to ensure that we have sufficient raw produce in the coming year to supply our own bakeries, food outlets and shops. We also work together to communicate everything worth knowing about the journey from field to bakery.

FRESH FLOUR

To bake tasty bread, you need high-quality flour, regardless of whether you're baking everyday brown bread or pastries for special occasions. When you buy flour, and especially when buying whole-grain flour with bran and germ, look closely at the best-before date, and make sure you get the freshest batch available. This will ensure the grains' aromas are still intact and that the fat contained in the germ has not yet begun to go rancid.

At Meyer's Bakeries, we mill our own whole-grain flour on a daily basis, and the enjoyment of baking with freshly milled flour is something we would encourage you to experience, too. You can either mill your own flour using a grain mill (see page 16), or buy freshly milled wheat or rye flour from local farmer's markets and even from the bulk bins found in some health food shops. As long as there is a high turnover of sales, flour sold in bulk should be very fresh. You might even be able to find some of the ancient or heritage wheat types, such as emmer, einkorn, spelt or kamut.

BREAD EVERYWHERE

When I think about how important baking has always been to me, I'm a little surprised that I didn't open the first Meyer's Bakery until 2010. On the other hand, I've barely had time to look back since. Today, we have five bakeries spread across Copenhagen as well as two locations in New York, one at the Great Northern Food Hall, and the other in Williamsburg, in Brooklyn.

And then we have a recurrent popup bakery at the huge music festival in Roskilde, Denmark. We make sure that those who have had a rough and rocking night get some colour in their cheeks with freshly baked, wonderfully aromatic rolls, and a special roast pork sandwich with red cabbage, mustard dressing, raw apples and pickled cucumber, all served in an organic bun made from our own Øland wheat.

Our project was never about selling as many loaves of bread as possible. It's about contributing to an enjoyable, healthier, tastier and more sustainable bread culture. And so we do whatever we can to share our knowledge with others. Each month, we host lots of baking classes. We offer both short, concentrated or longer, extended classes. A couple of times each year, we host huge workshops and popup baking schools with as many as 1000 participants, for both children and adults. We also occasionally host masterclasses with internationally renowned, phenomenal bakers including Chad Robertson and Melissa Weller.

In collaboration with the Danish Prison Service, some of the inmates in our prisons are all taught how to bake. The Melting Pot Foundation, which I founded in 2010, runs three food schools in three different prisons. We bring the inmates up to the exam that would gain them entry to a basic training course for chefs, we teach them how to make and take care of a starter, and we teach them how to bake. In one of the prisons, we have even established a professional bakery. From there, the aroma of freshly baked organic bread spreads across the entire facility. The inmates now bake their own bread every day, saving the prison close to 1 million Danish kroner (more than £116,000) every year.

We have another Melting Pot project in Bolivia, where we opened GUSTU in La Paz in collaboration with the Danish nongovernmental organization, IBIS. 'Gustu', meaning 'taste' in Quechua, the Incas' indigenous language, is a cookery school for impoverished and socially vulnerable young Bolivians, as well as a gourmet restaurant, bistro, and bakery. We train cooks, waiters and bakers, and we believe that this enterprise will help develop Bolivia's future food and restaurant industry and generate sustainable gastronomic projects in local communities all over Bolivia.

The bread produced at GUSTU is already very popular. One of their greatest successes is the *tantawawas* (a bread similar to brioche), which is shaped like babies and eaten on Día de Muertos (Day of the Dead), on 1 November, the Bolivian holiday celebrated in commemoration of dead relatives.

I hope that you will share your own experiences in life's great school of baking with someone you care about. Eating better bread (and preferably home-baked) is much more important than you may realize. Together we can move mountains.

CLAUS MEYER

Baking course at Meyer's House of Foodcrafts, Copenhagen.

A huge baking workshop in Kolding, Jutland, with 1000 baking enthusiasts

Per Grupe talks about different types of grains on a field walk

A mill in our bakery in Copenhagen's eastern borough

A thousand baking enthusiasts at a huge baking workshop in Roskilde

A baking course at Meyer's House of Foodcrafts, Copenhagen

American grain researcher Steven Jones talks about future-sustainable types of grain at a conference on biodiversity at Meyer's House of Foodcrafts

Starters, flour, juice, and marmalade on the shelves of our store in the centre of Copenhagen

Inside the kitchens at Jyderup prison

Festivalgoers using a starter to make bread at a pop-up baking workshop

Children baking fish and bread as part of their cookery classes

Claus Meyer talking about bread at a music festival in Roskilde

Kamilla Seidler and Michelangelo Cestari tasting the bread from the GUSTU baking school in La Paz, Bolivia

Our pizza specialist, Christian Scannagatta, in action at our store in Lyngby, Copenhagen

Pizza masterclass with Melissa Weller from Sadelle's in New York, at our bakery in Copenhagen's eastern borough

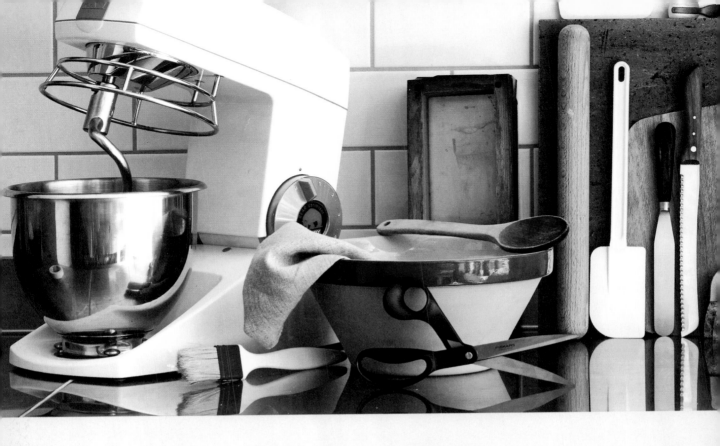

BAKING EQUIPMENT

You can buy lots of great, in fact, truly exquisite baking equipment. Some things you simply can't do without, while others just make baking more fun. Don't be concerned if you do not have a baking stone, even if it's listed under essential equipment. We'll provide you with alternatives that will enable you to get started with the equipment you do have, and you'll still get great results.

ESSENTIAL EQUIPMENT

OVEN

All ovens are different, which is why you should familiarize yourself with yours. Is the thermostat working? Does the oven bake evenly or one-sidedly? Whatever experiences you have with your own oven will not be the case with other ovens. When baking loaves and rolls, it's very important that your oven can get really hot, especially when you bake free-form wheat loaves. This is because they need initial extreme heat at the highest possible temperature for that perfect 'oven spring', when the dough puffs up in the first few minutes of hitting the hot oven. Bear in mind that you can't necessarily trust an oven thermostat because they can vary by as much as 25°C, So even if your oven shows 250°C, Gas Mark 9, it may in fact only be 225°C, Gas Mark 7. If you're unsure about how hot your oven can get, you can buy an oven thermometer. This also comes in handy if you are baking away from home as you can slip it in your back pocket before you go!

Make sure you give your oven plenty of time to heat up properly (at least 30 minutes) before you use it. If you have a baking stone, heat it along with the oven. It accumulates a lot of heat and if the stone is not at the desired baking temperature, your bread will not get the desired heat-shock. If you have a fan-assisted oven, use this function to heat up the oven and leave it on during the first few minutes of baking, as the oven will lose a little heat when you open the door to slide in the bread.

BAKING/PIZZA STONE

A baking stone is a fabulous tool for baking free-form wheat loaves. It mimics the conditions in a professional baking oven, where the bread is exposed to extreme heat from below as soon as it is

placed in the oven. This heat-shock causes the bread to swell up and become wonderfully light. Even dough that's over-risen, which would normally spread out, will be beautifully lifted thanks to the hot baking stone. Thick lava baking stones are particularly good in ovens that get really hot. Terracotta baking stones are less expensive and equally useful, though easier to break. But don't bin yours if it snaps in half, because it will still work just as well.

If you don't have a baking stone, you can place an ordinary baking sheet upside down in the oven and use that instead. When you are ready to bake your bread, simply slide the dough (on nonstick baking paper) onto the preheated baking sheet.

BAKING PEEL
A baking peel enables you to get free-form loaves in and out of the oven, and ensures that you don't burn your hands or cause the bread to collapse in the process. Many baking stones come with a plywood peel in the shape of a small spatula, which you can use to push the bread into the oven or onto the baking stone, either directly or on nonstick baking paper. If you don't have a baking peel, you can use the underside of a baking sheet. You could even use an appropriately sized piece of thick card, such as the lid of a pizza box. If you choose either of the latter two solutions, be sure to place the dough on a piece of nonstick baking paper first.

NONSTICK BAKING PAPER
is highly practical for many purposes; not least for pushing the fully risen loaves and rolls onto a baking stone or baking sheet. It comes in particularly handy when you bake bread rolls, as it makes placing the rolls in the oven all at once so much easier. Cut the baking paper to size to ensure it doesn't touch the sides of the oven.

A LARGE MIXING BOWL
When mixing dough with your hands or with a spoon, it's important to use a mixing bowl that's large enough to hold all the ingredients.

DIGITAL SCALES

It's really difficult to bake without good, precise digital scales you can reset to zero, not least when you have to measure small, precise amounts of, for example, yeast, sugar or salt. Choose a scale that doesn't reset too quickly on its own, which will allow you time to get all the ingredients ready. Digital scales are widely available in department stores or online and can cost less than £10. For the recipes in this book we recommend that you use gram measurements – even for liquids.

MEASURING IN MILLILITRES

When precise measurements are not absolutely essential, for example, when refreshing a starter, large amounts of liquids can be easier to measure in millilitres. It is helpful to have a measuring jug that ranges from at least 50 ml to 1 litre.

DOUGH SCRAPER

You will need a wide dough scraper (see pages 12–13) to tighten the surface of your dough after it has risen for wheat bread, baguettes and rolls (you can read more about how to tighten your dough on page 60). In fact, having two dough scrapers is a good idea, as you can use one to scrape the dough off of the other. (If there's any dough on the spatula you use for tightening it will stick, and then all hell breaks loose!) You also need to use a dough scraper to lift the dough onto the baking peel or nonstick baking paper. A dough scraper is also really handy for gently removing leftover dough – even when it's dried hard – from your work surface.

#TIP

You can buy dough scrapers, specifically for bread baking in any baking supplies shop. However, a regular metal scraper with a stainless steel blade of approximately 20–25 cm (such as a taping knife) from a DIY shop will be just fine.

A LARGE, FLAT WOODEN SPOON

This is ideal for mixing wheat or rye dough and for mixing cake batter.

RISING BOWL

To keep the dough moist, it's a good idea to use a sturdy plastic bowl with a lid when you need to let the dough rise in the fridge overnight. And using a transparent bowl is even better as it allows you to keep an eye on the dough without having to remove the lid. If you don't have a bowl with a lid, you can simply place a thin plastic bag or a cut-open freezer bag over the bowl and fasten it with an elastic band.

METAL BAKING TINS

We use these for baking rye bread, whole-wheat bread and for some of our pastries. They come with different nonstick coatings, but then you have to be careful not to scrape the coating when coaxing the bread out of the tin. We've used loaf tins that hold 1.5 litres for the rye bread and 2 litres for all other breads, but you can also use slightly larger sizes. If you're worried that your bread may stick to the bottom, you can always grease the tin and line it with nonstick baking paper, which is quite a foolproof way of getting your bread out in one piece. In some recipes, we use disposable tins, and you can usually buy these in supermarkets.

ROLLING PIN

We use a rolling pin for rolling dough thinly. A thin rolling pin is especially useful with delicate types of dough. Because you get better contact with the dough using a rolling pin, it stops you pressing down too hard.

A PLASTIC SCRAPER is useful

for scraping the rising bowl clean (use the round corners for this). The flat side can be used to spread pastry filling, for example.

A BRUSH is used to brush many

of the recipes in the enriched dough chapter with beaten egg, milk or water.

BAKING THERMOMETER

Thermometers are quite handy for checking when the bread is done. It's a great help when you bake wheat bread from wet dough, because it's not always easy to determine precisely when the bread is done. And the same goes for baking rye bread, as you can't simply tap the bread to find out if it's baked. Because ovens do not bake uniformly, which means varying baking times, measuring the core temperature (see page 288) is the most precise way of determining whether or not the bread is done. A baking thermometer is especially helpful the first few times you bake your own bread, and before you're experienced enough to assess when it's done simply by using your senses.

We recommend using a digital thermometer with a long probe. They are very precise and easy to read (and you can even use it when roasting meat or poultry). To get the most accurate reading, plunge the probe right into the centre of the loaf. In addition,

you can use the thermometer to check if any raw products you might be using are at the correct temperature.

#TIP

If you use a thermometer to check when the bread is done, it doesn't matter if you use a baking tin that's a different size than the one used in the recipe. A larger tin will require longer baking time, while a smaller tin requires less. However, if you stop baking your bread as soon as it reaches the right core temperature (you can check this with a kitchen thermometer, see page 288), you can be absolutely confident that it's done. Of course, you still have to keep an eye on the crust – you want it to be beautifully golden.

SERRATED BREAD KNIFE

Make sure the knife is so sharp it practically slides through the bread.

EQUIPMENT THAT MAKES BAKING MORE FUN

FOOD STAND MIXER

A food stand mixer will be quite useful, especially when working with wet dough that needs to be mixed more thoroughly and for longer than other types of dough. It'll save you both time and elbow grease. The market for stand mixers has genuinely boomed since manufacturers

have picked up on the growing interest in baking and have come up with lots of different models, both large and small. The mixer we used for the recipes in this book has a 5-litre bowl, but you'll be able to use most models for all our recipes. If you have a larger mixing bowl, you may want to double the recipe, and if it's a little smaller than the one we used, you can halve the recipe.

When making wheat bread, use the dough hook, and use the paddle for making rye bread. You should also be aware that all known models will jump a little when you mix wheat dough at high speed, so hold on to the machine to steady it. If left unattended, it might skip across the countertop and land on the floor.

#TIP

If the mixer starts to sound a little overworked, turn the speed down.

CASSEROLE POT FOR BAKING

Baking wheat bread in a deep, cast-iron lidded casserole is a really great idea because the casserole will support the dough and ensure it doesn't spread out, which can sometimes be a problem. A covered casserole also adds the natural moisture of steam, until you lift the lid. Of course, you need one with handles and a knob that are ovenproof. On some of the French

cast-iron casseroles, including Le Creuset™, you can actually unscrew the knob on the lid and replace it with a screw and ball-bearing to avoid steam escaping.

SCORING THE DOUGH

In some recipes, we suggest you score the dough, which will allow the bread to widen a little when it's placed in the hot oven. The best thing for this is actually an old-fashioned (unused) razorblade. Or, you can score the dough with a sharp pair of kitchen scissors or a really sharp knife.

A THIN SPATULA made of wood or silicone comes in very handy when you want to ease your rye and whole-grain bread from the baking tin without damaging the inside of the tin.

PROVING BASKETS (also called bannetons) are useful for some of our recipes, as it leaves a little pattern on the dough. We use proving baskets for the Grantoftegaard bread (see page 229) and the Levain bread (see page 232), among others.

SPECIAL EQUIPMENT

GRAIN MILL

Investing in a small electric grain mill can really save you money in the long run because you can mill your own flour exactly as needed, and you get to decide how fine you want your flour to be. In fact, the small ceramic stone-mills produce much finer flour than ready-milled flour, which has usually been processed on large stone-mills. The flour you mill yourself is whole-grain flour (read more about how to mill your own flour on page 35).

Most important, the flour you mill yourself will always be fresh. Flour is a delicate product because the grain contains wheat-germ oil, which quickly goes off. As long as it is sealed inside the germ the oil is protected so it will last almost indefinitely. But the moment you start milling the grains, the oil oxidizes and after some time, the flour goes rancid. Technically, you can bake with rancid flour (which a lot of people probably do unknowingly), but it does give the bread a slightly bitter taste.

This is similar to what happens to the taste of coffee made from beans that have been ground in industrial quantities and then allowed to go stale. Compare that with the taste of an espresso brewed with freshly ground beans!

If you shop around, it is possible to buy a kitchen-size electric grain mill starting from just over £100. A grain mill can also be purchased as an attachment for a large stand mixer, such as the Mockmill (see www.wolfgangmock.com/en/).You may be able to get extra equipment for some models, which will allow you to sift your flour after milling the grain. However, you can always use a wire sieve to sift the flour.

MEASURE INGREDIENTS BY WEIGHT
For the greatest accuracy and best results, we suggest you weigh all ingredients, including liquids. Please refer to the ESSENTIAL EQUIPMENT section for information about purchasing and using digital scales.

ORGANIC PRINCIPLES

In Meyer's Bakeries, we only use organically grown flour from northern Europe, because we believe that organic farming is the future, both locally and globally.

Most of the grain we use comes from the Danish island of Zealand. There, the different types are grown in rotation with broad beans, clover and lupine because these crops naturally add nitrogen to the soil, which fertilizes our grain. Furthermore, animal manure is added to the soil, which ensures that there is enough nitrogen to yield a reasonable crop and that the different types of grain maintain a high level of protein, resulting in higher gluten qualities. Each year, we calculate how many different varieties we need to grow and how much, and then we arrange the production with approximately 10 farmers. We're also deeply involved in the running of a century-old mill in Skåne, Sweden, where the grain that we do not mill ourselves (in the bakeries) is milled. We are the mill's single major purchaser. In terms of growing and milling different types of grain, we do so only in close collaboration with farmer, grain expert and organic pioneer, Per Grupe at Mørdrupgård.

GRAINS WITH AND WITHOUT CHEMISTRY

Organically farmed grain does not contain pesticides and is not fertilized artificially. It's grown using the same method that dates back to the very origin of grain growing, and until just over one hundred years ago, it was the only method used in farming. However, that all changed as more mouths had to be fed, and the industry developed new technology to increase crop yields.

This meant that grains that grew in just about any and all conditions – with the addition of the right amount of chemicals – replaced flavourful, nutrient-rich indigenous grains. Yields increased with this new type of grain, and the farms themselves expanded. However, as science pushed ahead, the practical knowledge that had guided farming for thousands of years was forgotten and the habit of growing better-tasting, nutritious grains was abandoned. Because their yield was much lower than modern types, the precious heritage wheat grains were phased out.

HERITAGE GRAINS AND MODERN ORGANIC FARMING

Heritage wheat grains, such as spelt, emmer and einkorn, as well as the old types of wheat found in Øland and Halland in Sweden, are much more robust in terms of disease resistance than modern types of wheat. The grains are better at utilizing the nutrients from the soil and can resist competition from other weeds or crops better than modern types of grain. This applies to the heritage wheat types grown in the UK, too.

Growing conditions for organic and biodynamic crops may be reminiscent of the days before artificial fertilizers and modern chemistry. But in today's organic agriculture, farmers have developed cultivation methods that increase yields, and now harvests equal 50 to 75 per cent of those found in conventional farming. This also explains why organic flour and breads made from it have become more widely available and reasonably priced these days.

BEING MINDFUL OF THE GROUND WATER

For every 1 kilogram of organic flour you use when baking, or each time you buy about 2 kilograms of organic bread, you protect 300 litres of ground water from being contaminated by pesticides. So, baking with organic flour is not just important for the quality of bread you bake and your own health, it is also important for our shared planet. We have calculated that in one of our bakeries alone, we use approximately 435 tons of flour each year. That means we are protecting almost 145 million litres of ground water from contamination.

GRAIN

When you bake bread, the flavour, lightness or density, colour and nutrient level all depend on the grains you use in your flour, and on how many coarse bits of grain you leave in. On the following pages you'll find a summary of the four most common Danish cereal species (wheat, rye, oats and barley) as well as the primary species and varieties we use in our bakery here in Denmark. We look at their strengths and weaknesses, and what it all means to the bread you bake.

SPECIES AND VARIETIES

We differentiate between their species and varieties. Wheat, rye, oats and barley are different species. Within the wheat family, there are different varieties such as einkorn, emmer, spelt, and wheat. The wheat that originates from Øland and Halland in Sweden are examples of different strains that all belong to the same wheat varieties.

SPECIES	WHEAT VARIETIES	EXAMPLES OF STRAINS
Wheat Family (divided into wheat varieties) →	Einkorn	
	Emmer	
	Spelt	
	Wheat →	Øland wheat
		Halland wheat
		Dalar wheat
		Purple wheat berries
		Dacke
Rye →		Slash-and-burn rye (*svedjerug*)
Oats		
Barley		

DIFFERENT VARIETIES – DIFFERENT QUALITIES

Each species includes numerous varieties, each with their distinctive qualities, as we know from apples, potatoes and strawberries, for example. Wheat, rye, oats and barley all have lots of varieties with grains of different sizes and colours, each with their distinctive flavour and baking qualities. In the same way as Granny Smith and Cox's Orange Pippin are two varieties of apples with their own distinct qualities, Øland wheat and Dacke each impart a different aroma and density to a finished loaf of bread.

YIELD OR TASTE

In the old days, it was important to ensure the highest possible yield from each harvest, enabling the farmer to feed both family and livestock. A bad harvest could prove fatal, and so the luxury of contemplating flavour quality was not really an option. High and consistent yields were what mattered and those factors influenced what was planted. Denmark is located right on the northern frontier of edible-wheat farming, which is why the majority of grains grown here are used in animal feed rather than for human consumption.

These days, it's still the question of high and consistent yields year after year that proves decisive for developing new and commercial varieties of grain for baking. This is why, in conventional farming, financial considerations determine that grain varieties with a lower yield but higher baking quality and better taste are less feasible, and so they're overtaken by varieties with a higher yield.

SCANDINAVIAN GRAIN PIONEERS

Fortunately, there are pioneers in the field, such as Hans Larsson, Anders Borgen and Per Grupe who, aided by the Nordic Gene Bank, have discovered that many of the heritage grains are really tasty and have great baking qualities. They test old grain types, preserved at the Nordic Gene Bank, by sowing small portions of grain and cultivating them for a few years, until they find out which of the different grains can be used in contemporary farming.

....

NORDIC GENE BANK is a Nordic institution aimed at the preservation of genetic plant resources. It collects and preserves different types of plants to ensure that we'll be able to reintroduce the various plants in the future and to log their history. Currently, the Nordic Gene Bank holds more than 30,000 different types of plants.

....

Not all heritage grains are equally useful, but every now and again, the pioneers make a particularly good find among the 600+ types of grain they have tested. Such grains may not provide the highest yield, but they taste great, are nutritious and are highly suited to organic farming. This also means that slowly but surely, more and more heritage grains find their way into grocery stores and supermarkets. Both Øland wheat (which we are quite partial to at Meyer's Bakeries) and *svedjerug* (slash-and-burn rye) are useful examples. Another great example is spelt, which was all but forgotten. However, now it's once again an everyday household item (not least thanks to Jørn Ussing from Aurion) and it is highly appreciated on account of its slightly different taste and because it's easier to digest than many modern wheat sorts. New sorts on our horizon include Halland wheat and Dalar wheat.

THE PRICE OF TASTE

Flour made from rediscovered heritage grains is often more expensive than regular, organically grown wheat or rye flour, simply because of the lower yield. However, today there are consumers who are willing to pay a little extra for the good taste, high baking qualities and the story behind the flour.

WHEAT VARIETIES

The progenitor of every cultivated wheat variety is einkorn; an ancient wheat that dates back to around 10,000 B.C.E. In the wild, einkorn crossbred with other varieties, which have evolved into the wheat variety known as emmer. Emmer also crossbred naturally with other wheat varieties. This gave the wheat-growing world spelt, which also crossbred with other varieties and gave us the variety of wheat we are familiar with today.

EINKORN → EMMER → SPELT → WHEAT

EINKORN

Einkorn is the oldest cultivated wheat variety known today, but it was completely absent for many years. This is a shame because einkorn has a lovely sweetness to it and a delicate flavour similar to fresh hazelnuts. The gluten quality in einkorn is very soft, which means it is more suitable for breads baked in a tin than for free-form loaves. For an even better result, we blend it with common wheat to maintain the great taste of einkorn while strengthening its gluten quality and thus adding a little lightness (see recipe on page 129). You can buy einkorn grains or flour online, or in health food shops.

EMMER

Emmer is the wheat variety that came after einkorn. From 5,000–4,000 B.C.E. it was one of the most important grains in Denmark. Emmer has a firmer core than einkorn, which makes it a little easier to use in baking, but we also blend emmer with common wheat to give the bread a lighter quality. Emmer imparts a slightly darker crumb as well as a lovely aromatic flavour (see recipe on page 126). You can buy emmer online or in health food shops.

SPELT

Spelt will give you an aromatic and tasty loaf of bread and up until medieval times, it was the preferred grain variety in Denmark. One of the reasons farmers throughout the world had switched from spelt to common wheat was the extra layer of chaff on spelt grains. This meant more work to remove it, which was a substantial obstacle in the days when the job of removing the chaff from the grain was done manually.

Spelt is the heritage wheat variety with the best baking qualities, except that its gluten quality is not as firm or as expansive as that of common wheat. When you use spelt, don't be too heavy-handed and don't mix the dough for too long or else you may end up with dough that's so soft and slack it might fall apart (see recipe on page 125).

Spelt has a high protein and vitamin content and people who are wheat intolerant will often fare better with spelt (as well as the rest of the heritage wheat varieties). Spelt flour is now widely available in regular supermarkets and grocery stores.

COMMON WHEAT

Compared to rye, barley and oats, common wheat is the grain variety with the best baking qualities. Thanks to its high gluten content, it yields an elastic, supple dough, and bread with an open crumb. When you purchase a bag of flour, and it only states wheat flour on the package, it is most likely a mixture of different species of modern wheat, blended by the miller in a ratio that provides the optimum qualities.

The common wheat variety we currently prefer to use at Meyer's Bakeries is called Dacke. It's a modern Swedish variety that's 'only' 20 years old. It works well in organic farming, and its flavour, texture, yield and protein qualities are equally well balanced. We use this modern wheat flour as the basic flour in many of our recipes, and then blend it with other wheat strains or some of the heritage wheat varieties, as well as the rural varieties.

SPRING AND WINTER WHEAT

Another subcategory of wheat is spring and winter wheat. Spring wheat is sown in spring (hence the name) and has higher protein levels than winter wheat, which is sown in late autumn. In our flour blend, we use mainly spring wheat along with just a little winter wheat. Both spring and winter wheat are harvested in August.

THE OLD RURAL VARIETIES

We have become quite fond of the old rural varieties in Meyer's Bakeries. These heritage wheat varieties adapt easily to the places they are grown, and in this way are more versatile and diverse than modern types of wheat. At the same time, their gluten quality is softer, which makes them easier for many people to digest. Modern types, in comparison, usually have a much higher gluten quality and are therefore more difficult to digest. In fact, some people are even allergic to modern types of wheat. The rural varieties are often named after the places where they were first cultivated.

Unfortunately, none of the Danish heritage wheat strains have been preserved, but we do have quite a few of the Swedish heritage grains. When you buy Øland wheat, the name refers to the wheat strain. Most of the Øland wheat we use and sell at Meyer's Bakeries and in Coop's supermarkets is grown in Denmark and not in Sweden.

ØLAND WHEAT

Øland is our favourite wheat strain and, as the name implies, it originated on the Swedish island of Øland. Up until the middle of the 1990s, it was a forgotten strain, and was only available in the shape of frozen seeds in the Nordic Gene Bank, which is where grain researcher Hans Larsson found them. He planted a few and thus set off the new cultivation. He gave a handful of seeds to the Danish farmer Per Grupe – a collaborator with Meyer's Bakeries on the development and cultivation of grains for flour – and the seeds were sown on his land at Møldrupgård in North Zealand, Denmark. The Øland wheat adapted so well to the local climate and soil that one small handful has turned into large fields spread across the entire country, resulting in lots of flour, and lots of lovely bread.

Øland wheat has a unique sweetness and a characteristic taste. It also contains high levels of protein and gluten. This results in dough with a high level of hydration and, as long as the dough is handled properly, yields bread with a tender, moist crumb and large, beautiful holes (see recipe on page 63).

DALAR WHEAT

Dalar wheat comes from the district in Sweden called Dalarna. As was the case with many of the heritage wheat strains, it was almost completely forgotten. However, seeds were kept in the Nordic Gene Bank, and these have now been rediscovered. And once again, Hans Larsson was instrumental to Dalar wheat's revival. It has a deep, sweet taste and its baking qualities are much on par with Øland wheat. In addition, Dalar wheat contains a high level of iron and magnesium (see recipe on page 97).

HALLAND WHEAT

Halland wheat is from Halland in Sweden. It has a delicate, nutty taste and its baking qualities are quite similar to Øland and Dalar wheat.

PURPLE WHEAT BERRIES

Purple wheat berries contain the same natural colouring agents found in cherries and grapes, and leaves bluish-red nuances in the finished bread (see recipe on page 94). The purple wheat berry grain distinguishes itself by the number of different antioxidants it contains. Purple wheat berries have a lovely flavour and with their high level of starch, they give the bread a more dense structure than bread made from other wheat varieties.

RYE

Since the time of the Vikings, rye has been the preferred grain for Danes. Rye is perfect for the damp and cool summers as well as the lean soil you find in Nordic countries. It became popular to grow rye because it provided a more stable and consistent crop than wheat, which is much more dependent on sunshine and warm summers.

Rye flour gives off a slightly alkaline and metallic scent, but when it's treated with tender loving care and baked along with a rye starter, it develops a fabulous deep aromatic flavour as well as a lovely dark crumb. On top of this, rye also contains high levels of fibre, vitamins and minerals. Perhaps this makes it easier for others to understand why most Danes miss their rye bread so much when they go abroad.

The gluten quality in rye is a little different from that in wheat and so it does not create strong gluten bindings the way wheat does. Furthermore, rye contains a high level of pentosan, a vegetable gum that breaks down the gluten structure. Fortunately though, pentosan also binds some of the carbon dioxide that's generated as the dough rises, and in this way it actually secures a more open crumb in rye bread than would otherwise be the case. However, it goes without saying that you'll never get rye bread with a crumb that's anything like the crumb you get in wheat bread.

When you bake bread with mostly rye flour, you may experience different results depending on whether or not it's been a rainy summer or autumn. This is why it's so important to always use a starter when baking rye bread. See "Falling number" on page 278 for more information about how the summer climate can affect the grain harvest and ultimately the quality of flour.

SLASH-AND-BURN RYE

Also known as *svedjerug* this is an old rye strain named after the slash-and-burn agricultural methods once used in Norway, Sweden and Finland. Until the eighteenth century, farmers scorched or slashed and then burnt small forested areas. Minerals in the ash fertilized the soil, making it ideal for growing rye.

A few of the rye strains from these old farms were kept in the Nordic Gene Bank and re-introduced, though farmers no longer use the slash-and-burn method, which is now illegal. There are significant differences between common rye and slash-and-burn rye. Slash-and-burn plants grow taller, as high as 2.5 metres, yet the seeds are only half the size of common rye seeds. The number of nutrients is much higher in slash-and-burn rye, which has a protein content in the region of 15 per cent, as opposed to 9 per cent in common rye.

Slash-and-burn rye has become quite popular in Denmark, even though its yield is much lower than modern rye strains, and this is not least due to its taste. Bread made from slash-and-burn rye has a particularly mild and enjoyable flavour, and does not dry out as quickly as bread made from common rye (see recipe on page 159).

OATS

Oats have been cultivated in the Nordic countries since the Bronze Age, and it thrives in our cool, damp climate. Norwegian scientists have revealed that oats grown in our climate develop a higher concentration of all the important substances than oats grown in warmer climates. Similar to einkorn, emmer and spelt, oats are difficult to shell before milling, which is why oat flour is more expensive than wheat flour.

Oats are distinguished by having more than double the fat content of rye, wheat or barley. And just like barley, the fibre content is sky-high, which gives oats a cholesterol-reducing effect. Oats also contain an even higher level of essential amino acids. This is also why oat flour quickly becomes rancid, so don't keep it on the shelf for too long. Oats are probably best known as rolled oats, which are, of course, quite delicious in biscuits (see recipe on page 249). When you use oats for baking bread, you'll get a lovely sweet, nutty-flavoured loaf. However, oats contain no gluten proteins, so you'll need to use at least 50 per cent wheat flour if you want an open crumb. On page 98, we provide you with the recipe for our delicious and moist new bread, where we use both oat flour and oat porridge in the dough.

BARLEY

Barley is one of the oldest grain species we know of and it thrives in cool northern climates. It has a significantly higher content of essential amino acids than either wheat or rye, and eating barley is believed to have a cholesterol-reducing effect.

Here in Denmark today, we primarily use barley for pigs' fodder or as malt for brewing beer. However, there was a time when barley and rye were a staple food for most Danes, while the wealthy enjoyed the more exquisite and expensive wheat.

Barley has a sweet flavour, but it also has an interesting hint of bitterness to it, too, which is detectable in bread baked with barley. Barley flour is difficult to use on its own, as it is not high in gluten. This means you have to mix the dough for a long time, as the flour is slow to hydrate, and the resulting bread is rather sticky. However, if you use 50 per cent barley flour and 50 per cent wheat flour, you'll get bread that places itself in an interesting middle position between wheat and rye bread (see recipe on page 130), with a very distinctive colour and aroma. Naturally, you can also use barley flour to spruce up your wheat bread, and as long as you replace no more than 20 per cent of your wheat flour with it, you should have no problems.

Common barley must be shelled before milling. However, the barley grown by Per Grupe, which we use in Meyer's Bakeries, is the naked barley variety. As the name implies, it has no outer layer of bran.

FROM GRAIN TO FLOUR

Before the grain can be used to bake bread, it must be turned into flour. The three most important parts of the grain are:

ENDOSPERM – the inner, white part, contains protein and starch. This is where the flour's gluten content is located.

GERM – the dark yellow part of the grain at the bottom. This is the grain's 'embryo' and it contains protein and fat.

BRAN – the outer shell that surrounds the germ and endosperm. This contains fat, fibres and vitamins.

WHEAT GRAIN

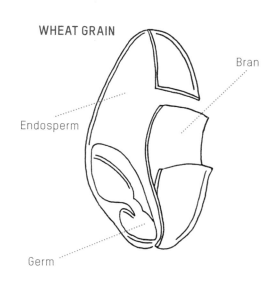

Bran

Endosperm

Germ

MILLING

The flour you buy may contain different levels of endosperm, germ and bran. This will depend on the milling process, which determines how much of the original whole grain is left in the flour, and how finely the flour is then sifted. For example, 100 per cent extraction indicates the inclusion of the entire grain, including endosperm, germ and bran, while 85 per cent extraction means that 85 per cent of the grain is included and 15 per cent of the coarsest bran and germ (the most nutritious parts of the grain where its flavour is also primarily located) has been sifted out. With 70–75 per cent extraction, all bran and germ are sifted out and only the endosperm remains. So, the lower the extraction, the greater the amount of coarse bits that have been sifted out, leaving the flour less flavourful and containing fewer nutrients.

STONE AND STEEL

The two most common ways of milling flour are by using a stone-mill, which is the ancient, original method, or by using a roller mill made of steel. Today, flour is primarily ground using fast roller mills.

GRINDING FLOUR USING ROLLER MILLS

When milling flour in a roller mill, the bran and germ are removed from the grain, leaving only the endosperm, which is then ground into 'pure' white flour. This is the kind of flour we usually buy in supermarkets. It has a 70–75 per cent extraction, and contains far fewer vitamins, minerals and secondary nutrients.

When using a roller mill to make whole-grain flour, the bran and germ are added back into the white flour.

STONE-MILLED FLOUR

Stone-milling flour involves milling the entire grain between two stone slabs, without removing the bran and germ first. After milling, some of the bran and germ are sifted out of the flour in order to achieve a lower extraction. But because the entire grain has been ground, there will invariably be bits of bran and germ left behind in the flour. This is why even the finest stone-milled flours will contain a minimum of 80 per cent of the original grain, compared to the 75 per cent that results from grinding flour in a mill made of steel. The colour of stone-milled flour is often creamy yellow, and its flavour is a little stronger. In addition, the resulting flour is healthier because it contains more bran and germ, which are the sources of the grain's vitamins and minerals.

FLOUR'S RISING ABILITY

Sifted flour from a stone-mill does not rise as well as sifted flour from a roller-mill, because the small bran and germ particles 'slice' the gluten structure, making it less stable. However, if you wish to bake for, example, a heritage-wheat bread (see recipe on page 63) using only stone-milled flour, but want to maintain the bread's rising power, simply reduce the amount of whole-grain flour a little and increase the amount of sifted stone-milled flour accordingly. This will ensure an extraction and a rising ability on par with the combination of stone-milled flour and roller-milled flour, yet you will retain the flavour and high level of nutrients found in stone-milled flour.

DURABILITY

When stored properly, whole grains will last virtually forever. However, as soon as whole grains are crushed or milled into flour, the oil from the bran and germ is oxidized and it starts to become rancid. This means that the higher the extraction (in other words, the more bran and germ left in the flour) the more important it is to use the flour while fresh to ensure the best flavour.

So, be sure to use whole-grain flour that is as fresh as possible. The stone-milled flour we sell in our bakeries is never more than one week old, so it is always extremely fresh. If you buy whole-grain flour in grocery stores or supermarkets, check the production date to ensure that the flour is not several months old (reaching for one of the bags at the back of the shelf can sometimes prove wise). Sifted wheat flour from grinding mills contains no bran or germ, so the bits that become rancid have been removed. This is why, generally speaking, this type of flour lasts a lot longer.

You should always store flour in a dry, cool place, at no more than 10°C, and never in the company of strong-smelling foodstuffs, as flour may absorb other flavours.

MILL YOUR OWN FLOUR

If you want to mill your own whole-grain flour, to ensure freshness and the best possible flavour, buy a small grain mill for home use. The dimensions are usually no greater than about 15 x 15 x 30 cm. There are two ways to use home-milled flour:

• You can use your whole-grain flour to bake 100 per cent whole-grain bread or you can add a little sifted store-bought wheat flour to the recipe, when a combination is required.

• You can use a sieve with a fine mesh to get rid of some of the coarser bits in your whole-grain flour, to gain an approximation of the extraction you are aiming for. Remember that there will invariably be leftover bran and germ in your flour, so it cannot strictly be compared with regular wheat flour.

TYPES OF FLOUR	EXTRACTION
Regular wheat flour, ground on a mill made of steel and sifted	70 to 75 %
Stone-milled wheat flour	about 80 %
Whole-grain wheat flour, stone-milled or from a grinding mill	100 %
You can usually get einkorn, emmer, spelt and most of the heritage wheat strains as stone-milled wheat, or as stone-milled whole-grain flour.	
Rye flour, stone-milled or from a mill made of steel	100 %
Barley flour, whole-grain	100 %
Oat flour, whole-grain	100 %

STARTERS

WHAT IS A STARTER AND WHY IS IT SO USEFUL IN BAKING?

A starter is a natural culture in the form of a small portion of dough (runny or thick), which you reserve each time you bake. If cared for properly, its longevity is almost infinite. Bread baked with a starter has an absolutely lovely flavour. In addition, a well maintained natural starter is all you need to make your bread rise, though you can always add a little baking yeast, if needed.

A starter is one of the crucial ingredients of the bread we bake at Meyer's Bakeries. It imparts all types of bread with a refined acidity that cuts the sweetness of the grain and adds an extra layer of aroma. Furthermore, a starter prolongs the durability of your bread and it gives it a more expansive crumb.

In this chapter, we prepare you for baking with a starter. Using simple diagrams, we'll explain the processes that occur in a starter, and we'll provide you with a recipe for a wheat starter to be used in your wheat and whole-grain bread, as well as a rye starter for baking rye bread.

Of course, you can skip the theory and still bake absolutely wonderful loaves of bread with a starter. Then again, you might want to know what actually is going on in that mystical mixture of flour and water.

STARTER MYTHS

A lot of mystique and anxiety surround the idea of using a starter. It's reputedly difficult to work with and it's supposedly high-maintenance, and that's usually enough to stop most people from going any further with the idea. However, as soon as you get a sense of the processes that occur in your starter, and understand how easy it is to store and prepare it for baking, I have no doubt that you will use it and that the pleasure you find in baking will reach a whole new level. And once you discover that nothing involving a starter really has to be excruciatingly precisely measured and that you don't have to slavishly follow our exact measures, you'll feel much more relaxed about the whole thing.

WHAT GOES ON IN A STARTER?

Mixing flour and water creates a starter and in the mixture you'll find lactic acid bacteria and natural wild yeast cells. The wild yeast cells are primarily found in bran, but actually they're pretty much everywhere, including in the air and on our skin. Wild yeast cells are different from the baking yeast found in little packages in a supermarket, yet both function to make dough and bread rise.

When you mix flour and water and let the mixture stand for a while, several micro-organisms get to work and eventually make the mixture more and more acidic. Finally, the lactic acid bacteria will get the upper hand, and the resulting sour environment will 'awaken' the wild yeast cells in the flour, which have been in hibernation. The lactic acid bacteria and the wild yeast cells now share the available 'food' (the starch in the flour) as the lactic acid bacteria breaks down the starch and makes it into sugars that the wild yeast cells can digest. You could say that they exist in a kind of symbiosis within their own little ecosystem, where they also help each other drive out any bacterial competition. After a few days, the starter contains lots of lactic acid bacteria but not so many wild yeast cells. Because it is the wild yeast cells that are the leavening agents, you need to keep their numbers high in the starter. This is simply achieved by 'feeding' the starter with more water and flour. And the more times you do this, the greater the concentration of wild yeast cells will be.

USING A STARTER ON ITS OWN OR SUPPLEMENTED WITH A LITTLE YEAST

If you use only a starter without any additional yeast to bake bread, you'll still get beautifully risen and open-crumbed loaves. For example, we only use a starter for our Grandtoftegaard bread (see page 229). It does require a starter that is completely up to scratch though, which means a high content of active wild yeast cells. However, you can also combine a starter with a tiny amount of baking yeast, to make a kind of semi-starter bread. We use this semi-starter procedure with our hydrated wheat and whole-grain doughs to make absolutely sure that our loaves rise beautifully, just in case the starter is not all it should be. We add a starter to various types of our dough more for its lovely acidity than as a leavening agent.

That said, we don't add baking yeast to our rye bread dough, because it rises more easily with a rye starter. However, if you're unsure whether or not your rye starter is sufficiently active, you can always add a tiny amount of baking yeast to your rye bread dough.

HOW TO USE A STARTER

We use a wheat starter in our hydrated wheat dough and whole-grain dough, and, as stated, rye starter in our rye bread dough. We prepare our starter for baking in much the same way, regardless of which type we use. It's worth noting that you can easily make a rye starter into a wheat starter and vice versa (see page 45).

If the starter has not been used for a couple of days, the number of active wild yeast cells will have decreased as the starter grew increasingly acidic. So, before we use our starter in our dough, we have to make sure that it contains enough wild yeast cells and that it's only mildly sour. We refresh the starter by adding flour and water to it 8–12 hours before adding it to the dough. This increases the production of yeast cells significantly, and at the same time 'dilutes' the level of acidity, which creates an elegant, mild sourness. We call this approach a two-step starter. And to make it easily comprehensible and to distinguish between the two different steps, we have also given the starter two different names, depending on where in the baking process it is used. For an explanation, see the diagram opposite.

STOCK STARTER

This is the starter that you've made, have bought, have been given or have saved from the last time you baked. You keep this stock starter until the next time you bake. If you don't intend to use your starter for a few days, keep it stored in the fridge.

YOUNG STARTER

When you decide it's time to bake, you'll have to refresh your stock starter with flour and water to turn it into what we call young starter. You divide young starter into two parts: some of it you use as a leavening agent in the dough you're making, and to give your bread that lovely sour taste; the remainder you store for the next time you want to bake – this will be your new stock starter.

A NOTE ON YEAST

The recipes in this book call for fresh organic baking yeast. As stated earlier, we recommend that you use digital scales set to grams to get the most accurate measurements for your ingredients, and this is especially true for yeast.

If you have difficulty getting hold of fresh organic baking yeast you can use dried instant yeast, and organic kinds are available online. If using instant yeast you will need a smaller quantity – the easiest way is to divide the fresh yeast by three. Alternatively use the following conversions:

Fresh baking yeast		Dried instant yeast
3 g	=	1 g
5 g	=	1.5 g
15 g	=	5 g
35 g	=	12 g
50 g	=	17 g

HOW TO GET YOUR HANDS ON A STARTER

Once you've decided you want to bake with a starter, you need to get your hands on an active specimen. There are several ways to do this:

• On page 44 we tell you how to make your own starter. It takes 4—5 days for a wheat starter and a little longer for a rye starter. But then you can also sit back knowing that you have singlehandedly created the micro-cosmos of life that's bubbling away in your starter container.

• Perhaps one of your friends is the proud owner of an active starter. People usually love to share their starters, so ask them if they would be willing to give some to you.

• You can buy a starter online.

USING A STARTER

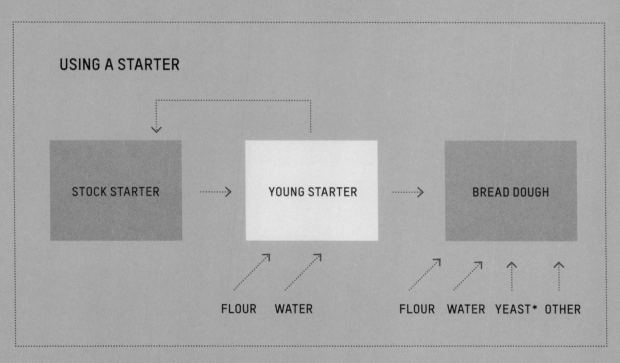

*You should only add baking yeast to rye bread dough if you're not certain that your starter is sufficiently active.

YOUNG WHEAT STARTER

The amounts we suggest below for refreshing a starter should suit most households. If you need more or less starter, you simply multiply or divide to fit the amount of bread you wish to bake. This way, you won't have to throw too much unused starter in the bin.

HOW TO REFRESH WHEAT STARTER

If you wish to refresh your stock starter to make young starter, you must begin 8—12 hours before you want to bake with it. Simply add flour and water to it in a ratio of 1 part stock starter, 2 parts water and 2 parts flour. Stir it with a wooden spoon – the starter should have a runny consistency – and leave at room temperature for 8–12 hours. Afterward, it's up to you what you do with the part of the stock starter that you didn't use to refresh your young starter. Perhaps you can share it with friends or you could use it to make tempura (see page 275), leaven flakes (see page 272) or simply put it in the bin. Regardless, you will have to get rid of your leftover stock starter one way or another, or else you'll end up with a huge batch on your hands.

YOU WILL NEED

50 g stock wheat starter
100 g lukewarm water
30 g wheat flour
30 g whole-grain wheat flour

1. Measure the stock wheat starter, water and two types of flour.

2. Add the stock wheat starter to a bowl and stir in the water. Add the two flours and mix well until smooth.

3. Leave the bowl at room temperature. The starter is ready to use when it starts bubbling slightly on the surface, tastes like a sour dairy product and smells like a mixture of honey, champagne and the foam of dark beer. This can take approximately 8 hours, but varies depending on how active your stock starter is and the room temperature. Now you have both your new young starter for baking and your new stock starter for next time you wish to bake.

The number of hours you can leave a young starter before using it is quite flexible, but ideally you should use it within 24 hours, otherwise it may become a little too acidic. Between 8–12 hours is the perfect time to use your starter because this falls between the time it starts to bubble and before the activity decreases too rapidly. Remember to reserve some of the young starter for your stock starter for next time you want to bake bread (see page 39 for more details).

YOUNG RYE STARTER

If young rye starter remains unused for more than a couple of days, it needs to be refreshed before it can be used to bake rye bread. Young rye starter needs to stand for at least 10 hours before being added to rye dough, as it should be more acidic and smell a little vinegary in comparison with young wheat starter.

YOU WILL NEED
150 g stock rye starter
300 g lukewarm water
195 g rye flour

2. Add the stock rye starter to a bowl and stir in the water. Add the flour and mix well until smooth. Follow the stock wheat starter method on page 40, but leave the young rye starter at room temperature for at least 10 hours before using it in your rye dough.

HOW TO MAINTAIN YOUR WHEAT AND RYE STARTER

If you bake regularly, you'll refresh your stock starter automatically, which will provide it with the nourishment it needs to stay in shape. However, if you keep your stock starter in the fridge, you will need to refresh it even if you are not actually planning to bake.

We recommend that you show your stock starter some loving care and attention by refreshing it once a month, even though it can actually survive longer unattended. Simply discard half of the stock starter before adding water and flour in a 1:1 ratio to yield approximately the same volume and texture. Shortly after, the starter will divide into a clear layer on top and a layer of flour at the bottom, but this is quite normal (see photo on page 49).

1. Measure the stock rye starter, water and rye flour.

HOW TO STORE STOCK STARTER

• Place in a plastic container or bowl with a lid.

• If you plan to use it within 2 to 3 days, leave the stock starter at room temperature then refresh it (see instructions opposite) approximately 8–12 hours before use.

• If you're not planning to use your stock starter within the next 4 days to 2 weeks, store it in the fridge. Take it out about 8–12 hours before you want to use it, refresh it, and leave at room temperature.

• If you're not planning to bake in the next 2 weeks or more, give the stock starter a little more flour to feed off. Add the flour a little at a time until the texture is like thick porridge and then place it in the fridge. Take it out 8–12 hours before use, refresh, and leave at room temperature.

• If you want to lavish your stock starter with extra attention, you can also take it out of the fridge a day earlier and refresh it twice – leaving 8 hours between each time you refresh it – before you use it.

Warning Never store a starter sealed in a glass jar with an airtight lid. On rare occasions, a starter can develop enough carbon dioxide to exert high pressure inside the sealed container. An airtight lid will lock the expanding gas inside, where it may build up enough pressure to explode. It is always safest to store starter in a plastic container with a flexible lid.

WILD YEAST CELLS

As explained on page 37, the wild yeast cells found in a starter thrive on the types of sugar that lactic acid bacteria produce when they break down the starch in the flour. As the wild yeast cells consume these sugars, they split and multiply, doubling hourly. So, for example, after 6 hours, there are 64 times more wild yeast cells in your starter than there were at the beginning. During this splitting process, the wild yeast cells produce the carbon dioxide that will act as the leavening agent in your dough and bread.

As long as the wild yeast cells have food they will keep splitting and producing carbon dioxide, but as soon as they have devoured the available sugars, the splitting process slows down until it comes to a complete halt. At this point the wild yeast cells slowly die over a longer period of time (see the graph opposite). When you make your starter by mixing water and flour, there are hardly any wild yeast cells, but after being refreshed with fresh flour and water four to five times in relatively rapid succession, there will be enough wild yeast cells to make any loaf rise properly.

Lactic acid bacteria found in a starter produce both lactic and acetic acid, which generates the sourness in the starter, and then awakens the wild yeast cells. The lactic acid bacteria produce three to four times more lactic than acetic acid, but the acidic ratio varies, depending on the starter's thickness and the surrounding temperature.

The warmer the temperature and the thinner the starter, the more the ratio between lactic and acetic acid favours lactic acid. The colder the surrounding area and the thicker the starter, the higher the level of acetic acid.

We are very fond of the taste generated by lactic acid bacteria, which is wonderfully mild and fresh, while the acetic acid is a little sharper and tends to dominate. All the same, we would like to maintain just a little acetic acid in our starter, as the taste of lactic acid can seem a little

WHAT HAPPENS IN YOUR STARTER WHEN IT'S REFRESHED

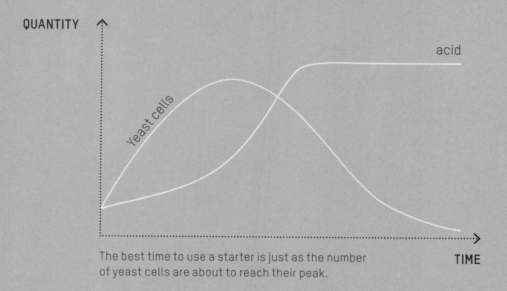

The best time to use a starter is just as the number of yeast cells are about to reach their peak.

metallic if it's not balanced by acetic acid.

This gives the impression that the warmer the starter's surroundings and the softer it is, the better the starter. However, under these circumstances, the lactic acid bacteria will work much faster and thus 'spit out' so much acid that the combined level of acid in the starter rises quite rapidly, which allows the taste of the acetic acid to dominate. This generates a sour and sharp taste that will drown out the taste of the lactic acid, even when the ratio actually stands in favour of the lactic acid bacteria.

So, to obtain a mild and elegant starter – if you bake regularly

and refresh your starter often – don't make your starter too thick. You can leave it in a warm place, but not for too long. This is what we do when we refresh our stock starter to make young starter for our wheat breads.

If, on the other hand, you don't bake that often, make your starter a little thicker and store it somewhere cool to slow down the activity of the lactic acid bacteria. Granted, coolness will provide more favourable conditions for the acetic acid, but as all processes are slowed down in a thick and cool starter, it'll take quite a while for the starter to get really sour, and the wild yeast cells will also survive longer. A high level

of acetic acid is not really a problem, because your starter will have to be refreshed and placed in warm surroundings before you add it to your dough, and this will rebalance the acids.

A STARTER BEARS NO GRUDGES
Fortunately, a starter has a very short memory. Even if you leave it to its own devices in the fridge for months, it'll forgive you after three days out on the kitchen table and with daily refreshing sessions.

HOW TO MAKE A STARTER FROM SCRATCH

Whether you want to make wheat or rye starter, the way you begin is the same. This process only needs to be done once, unless you're unfortunate enough to have your starter die on you (see page 49). Please note that, even if you are making a wheat starter, you need to use rye flour to start it (thereafter, you use only wheat flour to refresh a wheat starter). This is due to the fact that rye flour contains more of the micro-organisms needed to activate a starter.

YOU WILL NEED:
30 g bread flour or plain flour
30 g whole-grain wheat flour
30 g rye flour
150 g water

HOW TO MAKE A STARTER

1. Measure the water and three types of flours.

2. Add the three types of flour to a bowl. Add the water and stir until smooth.

3. Pour the mixture into a plastic container with a lid, but seal the lid loosely to begin with. Leave at room temperature for 4 days, and whisk it thoroughly once a day. After 4 days, bubbles should appear on the surface and it should taste a little sour. If it does not taste sour, leave it for another day or two.

MAKING A WHEAT STARTER

You can use your start-up wheat starter directly in the dough, but remember to reserve some to use as a stock starter next time you bake bread. The number of lactic acid bacteria will not be terribly high in a young starter, but it will increase after you use and refresh it a couple of times.

A New Starter → Young Wheat Starter

MAKING A RYE STARTER

To rise properly without the addition of baking yeast, rye bread needs more active wild yeast cells than a loaf of bread made from wheat flour. Leaving your young rye starter in warm surroundings and refreshing it every day for four to five days will provide the environment that will increase the growth of wild yeast cells to the level needed for baking rye bread.

A New Starter → Refreshing Rye Starter → Refreshing Rye Starter → Refreshing Rye Starter → Stock Rye Starter

The first time you refresh your starter, add 100 g of your new starter instead of rye starter, after which you follow the recipe on page 41. Each time you refresh your starter, throw (or give) away what you won't be using or you'll end up with far too much starter.

HOW TO TURN WHEAT STARTER INTO RYE STARTER – AND VICE VERSA

Starters are flexible and adaptable. Once they are up and running so to speak, you can easily turn wheat starter into rye starter and vice versa.

TURNING WHEAT STARTER INTO RYE STARTER

When your wheat starter is ready to use – having been refreshed a couple of times – it is easy to turn it into rye starter for baking rye bread simply by activating it a little more. Follow the instructions for refreshing a starter on page 41, but start with a wheat starter instead of rye. Let the rye starter stand at room temperature for approximately 24 hours. When it rises and starts to bubble on the surface, it is alive, kicking and ready to use for baking.

Stock Wheat Starter → Refreshing Rye Starter → Stock Rye Starter

TURNING RYE STARTER INTO WHEAT STARTER

It is quick and easy to turn stock rye starter into wheat starter. Follow the instructions on page 40, but use stock rye starter instead of stock wheat starter. You can actually skip a step and add stock rye starter to your young wheat starter, and then add the young wheat starter directly to your dough.

Stock Rye Starter → Refreshing Wheat Starter → Stock Wheat Starter

THE TYPES OF STARTER WE USE IN THIS BOOK

If you look at other baking books where they use a starter, you'll find that how a starter is used and refreshed, as well as the recommended intervals between refreshing the starter, vary. The texture of a starter can vary too. Some are thin, others very thick, and others again somewhere in between. You can use them all; they just work in different ways and yield different results. In this chapter, we've described how we make wheat and rye starter equivalent to those we use in most of the recipes in this book. However, in some of the recipes, we use other methods. See opposite for a list of the different starters included in this book.

WHEAT STARTER In most of our wheat breads we use a wheat starter combined with a little baking yeast. Here, the starter's most important role is to impart a delicate sourness to our bread, and it is less important as a leavening agent.

RYE STARTER Rye starter gives our rye breads a wonderful texture and lovely flavour. It not only imparts acidity to the dough but also acts as a leavening agent. While we do not add baking yeast to our rye breads, it's entirely possible to do so if you're unsure whether there are enough active wild yeast cells in your rye starter.

STARTER FOR 100 PER CENT STARTER-RISEN BREAD In our Grandtoftegaard bread (see recipe on page 229) we don't add baking yeast. For 100 per cent starter-risen bread like this, the starter needs to be a little thicker than a regular starter in order to increase its leavening powers. Refreshing the starter daily for at least three to four days before use will increase the levels of active wild yeast cells to enable the starter to act as the sole rising agent.

LEVAIN STARTER We use this for our Levain (see recipe on page 232). Soaking some organic raisins in water for five days is the way we start a levain starter. By adding the soaking water to the starter mixture the wild yeast cells from the raisins can be activated. Once they are active, we refresh our starter with flour and water in exactly the same way we do our regular starters.

APPLE STARTER This is actually more like a fruit yeast than a starter, and we use it for our wheat bread with apple starter (see recipe on page 235). When mashed organic apples (skin on but cored) are left to ferment for five to six days, wild yeast cells embedded in the apples' skin increase in number. When added to dough, the wild yeast cells eat the flour's sugar and go on to develop enough carbon dioxide to make the bread rise.

WHAT'S WRONG WITH MY STARTER – AND HOW DO I FIX IT?

Generally speaking, a starter is both adaptable and cooperative, but you may encounter problems along the way. Below, we take you through some of the more common issues and show you how to fix them.

MY STARTER APPEARS 'TIRED'

Your starter doesn't rise and bubble after being refreshed. It's become a little weak, and it needs 'muscling up' to obtain a higher concentration of wild yeast cells. To make it more active again, leave it at room temperature for three to four days, refreshing it daily. If that doesn't help, make a new starter (see page 44). Remember that as your starter starts to bubble after being refreshed, the bubbles will disappear again. This is quite normal because bubbles only occur as long as there is enough 'food' for the yeast cells and the lactic acid bacteria.

MY STARTER SMELLS RANCID

If your starter begins to smell slightly rancid, try refreshing it daily for three to four days, to see if that removes the bad odour. If this doesn't help, make a new starter (see page 44).

#TIP

You could make a new starter while also administering first aid to the starter that's giving off a bad odour. That way, you'll be sure to have a starter whether your rescue attempt succeeds or not.

MY STARTER IS SEPARATING

When your starter is left to its own devices, the flour will sink, leaving a thin layer of liquid on top and a thicker, sandy layer at the bottom. This is quite normal and no indication that anything is wrong with your starter. Just stir it from time to time, to make it smooth again.

MY STARTER IS VERY DARK ON TOP

Sometimes, the thin liquid on top of your starter may turn rather dark, especially if you've left it alone for quite a while. The dark colour is due to the alcohol produced as the starter ferments and is a sign that you need to refresh your starter. However, you shouldn't have to refresh it more then once or twice before it's up and running again.

SUMMER STARTER

In summer, your starter will become sour more quickly as all processes involved accelerate in warmer weather. If you use your starter on a daily basis or every other day, and you usually keep it at room temperature, leave it in the fridge during the day and then take it out and leave it on the kitchen table in the evenings in summer. If, however, you don't get to bake that regularly, keep it in the fridge and then, before using it, refresh the starter and leave it at room temperature for as long as you would normally do.

THERE'S MOULD ON MY STARTER

A starter is so acidic that it has an antibacterial effect, which would normally prevent mould bacteria from developing, and this is why your starter will never become mouldy inside. However, if you've splashed a little starter up the insides of the container you store it in, mould may grow there because dried starter is less acidic than wet, and cannot keep the mould bacteria at bay. The starter itself is fine though, so simply transfer it to another, clean container and continue to use it.

MY STOCK RYE STARTER HAS TURNED SLIGHTLY RED JUST BENEATH THE SURFACE

Your starter has been left for too long without being refreshed. So refresh it. When you are ready to use it for baking, it will benefit from being refreshed once more before making your young rye starter.

HAS MY STARTER DIED?

A starter usually tolerates neglect, so killing it is close to impossible. Usually, it'll simply be 'disappointed' or 'sour' and being refreshed daily three to four times normally brings back its kind and mild nature, full of active yeast cells that will help your bread rise. However, if you see no activity at all (no bubbles on the surface) after refreshing it a few times, then it may actually have passed away all the same. And then there's no way round it; you'll have to make a new starter (see page 44).

WHEAT BREADS

Combine the ingredients, mix, leave to rise, shape, then bake. It's that simple.

WHEAT BREADS

When I close my eyes and think of my ideal wheat bread, it is a rustic loaf with a moist and light crumb that is not noticably open, and it has a deeply dark crust that cracks as the bread is taken from the oven. It's a loaf of bread with profound, sweet flavours from freshly milled whole-grain flour that blends with the caramelized flavours of the crust and are cut by the slight tang imparted by a natural starter and a long cold fermentation. I have fantasized about this loaf of bread for the last 30 years. I have baked my way towards it with determination, and I have shared my thoughts on raw ingredients and the process of baking with just about anyone who showed an interest.

In 2006, I tasted a loaf of bread made by chef Erwin Lauterbach that had been made with Manitoba flour from Canada (with a pronounced high-gluten content), and I was impressed by the tender crumb, the lightness and the crisp crust. At the time, we had established our first bakery on Kattegatvej in Copenhagen's North Harbour. I'd employed bakers Nicolai Halken Skytte and Allan Salmi Sommer, and we were full steam ahead, challenging the myth that you cannot bake high-quality bread with Danish wheat, and most certainly not with organic wheat.

We quickly discovered that it was not a problem, as long as the grain we used contained a high level of protein and gluten. However, we also wanted to make bread that, compared to the Manitoba loaf, had a more explicit grain aroma, a somewhat more distinguishable sourness, a higher content of whole-grain and thus also

a slightly heavier crumb. Our efforts resulted in the loaf that is currently our most popular, sold at Meyer's Bakeries, namely the Øland wheat loaf. In fact, this loaf has inspired numbers of bakers to get better acquainted with the excellent qualities of the Øland grain. Along the way, we also changed our approach to baking considerably. Our dough became increasingly hydrated; we let it rise for much longer; we used a combination of a starter and a little baking yeast as leavening agents; and we mixed and shaped the dough completely differently.

Our way of baking differs greatly from the classical home-baking approach most of us are more familiar with where the dough is tougher, and you knead it directly on the kitchen table and then shape it with your hands. During baking it will rise to a predictable double size on the baking sheet. The method we introduce in the following chapter is a little more

like dancing or playing jazz. It demands greater attention, because you can never be quite sure what'll happen along the way. However, your reward, both in terms of effort and final product, will be all the greater for it.

In this chapter we provide you with our basic wheat bread recipe. First, we'll describe the ingredients you'll need, and then we'll share how to mix the dough and let it rise, and then how to bake your bread. All the recipes in this chapter are based on this fundamental dough, which you can then shape to your preference, as small or large loaves, baguettes, rolls, or pizza. You can also use other types of flour for variety or add seeds and flavourings to your dough.

HOW TO MAKE WHEAT DOUGH

1. Refresh your wheat stock starter 8–12 hours before use

2. Combine the water, starter, yeast, flour and salt, then mix

3. Leave the dough to rise for at least 12 hours

4. Shape the dough and bake it

STARTERS

You need a starter for your wheat bread. It will impart a better taste and a more extensive crumb, keeping the bread moist for longer. See how to make or get hold of a natural starter on page 39, if you don't have some ready for use.

REFRESH YOUR STARTER

To ensure that your starter is active as well as elegant and mild in taste, refresh it 8–24 hours before making your dough. Take your stock starter from the fridge or kitchen table, add water and flour (see page 40) and that's your young starter. Leave at room temperature and when it starts bubbling on the surface it's ready for use. It should also smell like a sour dairy product, like freshly brewed beer or like champagne.

#EMERGENCY SOLUTION

In an emergency, if you haven't had time (or simply forgot) to refresh your starter before baking, you can add 1 tablespoon of wheat stock starter or 1 teaspoon of rye stock starter directly to the dough. You won't get the same result in terms of taste and texture as when you use fresh starter, but even an unrefreshed starter will add character to your bread.

INGREDIENTS

WATER

You'll be using a lot of water. Handling 'wet' dough can be a little tricky as it tends to spread, but that's only until you get the hang of it. And you can always start off by using a little less water than mentioned in the recipe. This will make the dough easier to handle and you'll still get lovely bread with a tasty crumb that stays tender and moist for a long time (read more about hydration on page 284).

FLOUR

For our basic recipe, we use a blend of approximately 25 per cent whole-grain Øland wheat and 75 per cent regular bread flour. The whole-grain flour contains bran and germ where the flavours, vitamins and fibres are located. In other words, we add in all the good stuff.

You can replace Øland wheat with any other type of whole-grain flour. Ideally you should use a heritage wheat, such as emmer or spelt, because they have a sweeter aroma than many of our modern wheat varieties.

For this type of bread it is very important that the 75 per cent regular bread flour contains a high level of gluten. This ensures that the moist dough is able to contain the air that is produced as it rises, which yields a wonderfully light loaf of bread. If you choose flour with at least 12 grams of protein per 100 grams, you're almost guaranteed good gluten quality, but you're only certain once you've used the flour for baking. (Read more about protein content and gluten on page 280.)

As you become more and more confident with this type of wheat bread, you can choose to increase the amount of whole-grain flour you use. In fact, as much as 50 per cent of the total amount of flour used can be whole-grain without the final loaf losing its structure. However, the more whole-grain flour you add, the weaker and more fragile the gluten strands, which means that your crumb will be a little denser. In other words, a seriously healthy loaf of bread with lots of whole-grain flour and thus a wholesome flavour will also give you a denser crumb.

Of course, you can also choose to decrease the amount of whole-grain flour you use, which will give you a somewhat more open crumb and a milder flavour. Remember, though, that you must replace the whole-grain flour that you took out with exactly the same amount of regular bread flour.

YEAST

We bake our wheat bread using a combination of a tiny amount of baking yeast and a small quantity of starter. This is sufficient to ensure the bread won't taste too strongly of yeast but will rise perfectly. A starter, when it's allowed plenty of rising time in cool surroundings, will impart extra rising power to the bread, as well as a lovely flavour.

We recommend using fresh organic yeast because it contains a greater number of different yeast strains than conventional yeast, which adds more flavours to your bread. Furthermore, fresh organic yeast – unlike conventional fresh yeast – is not rinsed with chemicals during production and so is much less polluting. Instant yeast will also work fine – just add it to the flour before mixing. (Read more about yeast on page 282.)

SALT

We use regular fine salt because the finer the salt, the more easily it dissolves. As long as it's not too coarse, it doesn't matter whether you use cheap table salt from the grocery store, sea salt or Himalayan salt. In addition to adding flavour to both crumb but especially crust, salt adds texture to the crumb.

Technically speaking, you should use 1.2 per cent salt in relation to the final dough, i.e. water, a starter, yeast and flour. Some of dough's fluid will evaporate, so you will actually end up with 1.5 per cent salt once the bread is finished. But try adjusting the amount as you go along and add salt to suit your own taste. (Read more about salt on page 287).

THREE MIXING METHODS

FOOD STAND MIXER

A food stand mixer will mix your dough relatively quickly, in approximately 12–15 minutes. Your arms won't get tired and you won't break out in a sweat. However, using a machine means you may accidentally overdo the mixing, which is practically impossible if you mix by hand.

#KEEP AN EYE ON YOUR MIXER
We've mentioned this elsewhere in the book but it's worth saying again. There are many different stand mixers out there, and every single one of them will jump and dance across your work surface when mixing bread dough. So keep an eye on your machine to make sure it doesn't land on the floor. And if the motor starts to sound a little strained, give it a rest before finishing your dough.

1. Mix the cold water and starter in the mixing bowl. Add the yeast and stir until dissolved.

2. Add the flour and salt.

3. Attach the dough hook to the mixer, and set the mixer to the lowest possible speed for about 1 minute to gather the ingredients without flour flying all over the place.

4. When the flour has been incorporated turn up the speed to mix thoroughly. How long you need to mix the dough depends on the water-flour ratio, so don't look at your watch but keep an eye on the dough. When it slips completely off the sides of the mixing bowl and gathers round the dough hook, turn the mixer off immediately. Your dough is ready.

5. To ensure the dough is thoroughly mixed you can do a gluten test (see page 281). (You can read more about gluten on page 280).

BY HAND – THE QUICK METHOD

This method imitates a food stand mixer to some extent, only you use a flat wooden spoon. It may also be a good idea if you let the dough rest for half an hour before mixing it, a method known as autolyse. Read more about this on page 278.

Add the water and starter to a large mixing bowl. Then add the yeast, the two different types of flour and the salt. Mix, or rather beat, the dough with the wooden spoon, while scraping the dough off the sides of the bowl from time to time (this will allow air to seep into the dough). You should give it a good beating for approximately 10 minutes or longer, taking a few breaks, until the dough has transformed from a floury 'glue' to a smooth, shiny and supple dough that easily comes away from the inside of the bowl.

#TAKE TURNS

If you're baking with a partner, collaboration will only make your dough better since you can take it in turns to mix the dough while the other has a break.

#THE GLUTEN TEST

To check whether your dough has been mixed enough, lift a little of it and very gently pull it until it becomes somewhat like parchment. If you can stretch it thinly without breaking it, you have perfect dough that's ready to rise.

BY HAND – THE GENTLE METHOD

Using this method, you'll get a good feel for how the dough and gluten strands slowly develop. This method requires minimal strength but plenty of time. It takes approximately four hours in total, where you regularly show the dough a little attention by lifting it about once every half hour.

1. Put all the ingredients, except the salt, in a large plastic container with a lid.

2. Mix the dough by hand for approximately one minute.

3. Sprinkle salt on top of the dough and set the lid loosely on top of the container. Leave for 30–40 minutes. This part of the process is called autolyse and you can read more about it on page 278.

4. Place a small bowl with water next to your container. Dip your hand in the water and grab one corner of the dough. Carefully pull it upwards.

5. Pull the dough towards the opposite corner of the container and let go.

6. Give the container a one-quarter turn and repeat the procedure.

7. Keep turning the container and stretching the dough, four times in all. Loosely place the lid on top again and leave for another 30 minutes. Then repeat the entire procedure every 30 minutes, 6 to 7 times in all. You'll be able to feel how the dough becomes more and more expandable and supple with each time.

LET THE DOUGH RISE

USING DOUGH MIXED BY A FOOD STAND MIXER OR QUICKLY BY HAND

Oil the inside of a bowl or a plastic container. Transfer the finished dough to the container and place a lid or some clingfilm on top to stop it drying out. Make a mark showing how far up the dough is on the side of the container to help you keep track of how much it rises. The dough is now ready to rise.

Leave the dough at room temperature for about one hour. Then place it in the fridge for at least 12 hours, until it has approximately doubled in size. It may be a good idea to check on your dough a few hours before you want to bake your bread. If it hasn't risen sufficiently, you can take the container out of the fridge and leave it at room temperature for a few hours. The warmth will stimulate the yeast cells and the dough will rise to completion.

USING GENTLY MIXED DOUGH

The dough will already have risen to some extent while you were mixing it, so it only has to rise another 50 per cent in the fridge, once you've finished the mixing process. This should take 8–12 hours. If it hasn't risen sufficiently, you can take the container out of the fridge and leave it at room temperature for a few hours.

PREHEAT THE OVEN BEFORE SHAPING YOUR BREAD

It's important that the oven is extremely hot by the time the dough is ready to bake. Depending on how quickly your oven heats up, place your baking stone or pizza stone on the middle shelf and switch the oven on a good 30 minutes before you start shaping your bread. If you don't have a baking stone, you can get almost the same effect by placing a baking sheet upside down on the middle shelf.

SHAPING YOUR BREAD

Sprinkle plenty of flour on your work surface then carefully tip the dough out of its container onto it, without knocking the air out of the dough. Use one or two large baking spatulas to properly tighten the surface of your dough (see the step-by-step procedure on page 63). Brush flour on the side of the spatula you plan to use to tighten your dough. This keeps the outer surface taut and prevents the wet dough from clinging to it. Try to avoid trapping extra flour inside the dough because it can create unwanted pockets of flour in the finished bread.

#USE TWO DOUGH SCRAPERS

You can't stop dough clinging to your dough scraper as you tighten it, which is why it's beneficial to use two: one for scraping dough off of the other. This means you won't get clingy wet dough on your scraper and you won't find yourself pulling on the dough and deflating it.

BAKING YOUR BREAD

Now the bread is ready for baking. No extra rising time is needed since the dough is light enough as it is. Carefully lift your dough onto a piece of nonstick baking paper, using your spatula(s). Then gently slide the paper and dough onto the hot baking sheet or stone already in the oven. You can also use a baking peel or a large piece of card. Once you get the hang of it, you can lose the nonstick baking paper, but while you are getting used to handling bread dough this way it's easier than using a baking peel brushed with flour.

Bake your bread for approximately 5 minutes at the oven's highest temperature (250–275°C, Gas Mark 9–10). Then lower the temperature to approximately 230°C, Gas Mark 8. We say approximately, because ovens vary and they bake differently, which is why the actual temperature in your oven may be significantly different from our oven, and this influences the time it takes to bake a loaf of bread (read more about ovens on page 12). So, baking temperatures and baking times are approximations. You will need to use your senses (possibly aided by a kitchen thermometer with a probe, see page 12) to assess when your bread is done.

If the loaf sounds hollow when you tap it and it is nicely dark brown in colour, your bread is usually done. If you're not entirely sure, you can measure the bread's core temperature by sticking the thermometer's probe right into the centre of your bread. The temperature here should be 98–100°C.

When in doubt, it's better to bake your bread a little longer, but make sure you don't scorch the crust. Move the oven shelf up or down a level, depending on which position darkens the bread more. You can also reduce the heat or cover the bread with aluminium foil, or simply place a baking sheet between the bread and the heating element in the oven.

When done, transfer the bread to a cooling rack and leave to cool before slicing it. If you slice it the moment it's out of the oven you may well press down on it and ruin the texture. So, do your best to ignore temptation and be patient.

#FULL STEAM AHEAD

Place a roasting tin at the bottom of the oven and heat it along with the oven itself. As soon as you slide the bread into the oven, add about 100 g of water to the tin. Repeat after about 2 minutes. The water will turn to steam inside the oven, which will not only stop the bread's surface drying out but will help maintain the bread's moisture and elasticity early on in the baking process. This will allow the bread to expand more and more, increasing its overall volume, while its crust turns lovely and crisp.

STORING WHEAT BREAD

Wheat bread is best kept at room temperature. If you plan on eating your bread within a day or two, keep it in a paper bag. This will allow the bread to breathe and its crust to stay (reasonably) crisp.

If you don't expect to eat all of your bread in the next day or two, seal the portion you want to keep in a resealable plastic food bag and place it in the fridge. Then, when you want to eat your bread, you can heat it in a preheated oven at 200°C, Gas Mark 6. This will make it nice and tender again (you can even rub a little water into the bread before heating it, for extra effect). If you freeze loaves of bread or rolls, defrost them completely before heating them, also at 200°C, Gas Mark 6. (Read more about storing bread on page 286.)

A toaster is also useful if you want to enliven your bread, but make sure you don't burn it. Usually 10–20 seconds is sufficient to invigorate your bread, giving it a slightly crispy outside and a soft and creamy crumb.

#CRISPY CRUST OR TENDER CRUMB?

One of the few disadvantages of baking wheat bread with hydrated dough is that the crust softens after only a few hours. For a crispy crust you can add a little less water, but be aware that this will also make the crumb less tender.

OUR ØLAND WHEAT BREAD

The Øland wheat bread is my favourite, and our customers seem to feel the same way because our bakeries sell a huge number of Øland loaves. In fact, it's our best-selling loaf. And this makes us very proud since the bread encapsulates our entire philosophy of using a good natural starter and plenty of tasty Nordic whole-grain heritage flour to give the bread its distinctive character. The gluten quality in Øland wheat allows us to sufficiently hydrate our dough, yielding a really tender loaf, while imparting a nice, sweet flavour to the bread that goes incredibly well with the sour notes contained in a natural starter. The combination of plenty of water and Øland wheat ensures a tasty crust and tender crumb, the inside as soft as a doughnut, complemented by that lovely Øland wheat flavour.

If you cannot get hold of Øland wheat, don't worry. You can replace it with any whole-grain heritage flour, such as emmer or spelt or one of the rural varieties (see page 27), which all have a sweeter aroma than many modern wheat flours.

1 large loaf or 2 small ones

YOUNG STARTER
50 g wheat stock starter
100 g water
30 g bread flour
30 g whole-grain Øland wheat flour (or other whole-grain wheat flour)

DOUGH
550 g cold water
50 g young starter
5 g fresh organic baking yeast
150 g whole-grain Øland wheat flour (or other whole-grain wheat flour)
450 g bread flour
15 g salt

YOUNG STARTER
Refresh your stock starter approximately 8 hours before use (see page 40). Mix the ingredients in a small bowl with a removable lid, cover loosely, and leave at room temperature. The portion of the young starter you don't use will now become your stock starter, so save it for the next time you want to bake bread (see figure on page 39).

DOUGH
See pages 55–60 for instructions on combining the ingredients, mixing the dough and leaving it to rise.

#TIP
You can use common whole-grain flour if you can't get your hands on a whole-grain heritage variety, but go for the highest possible protein content (read more about the protein in flour on page 281).

HOW TO SHAPE THE DOUGH

1. Sprinkle plenty of flour on your work surface and carefully tip the dough out of its container without knocking the air out of it. Use a dough scraper to fold the dough over once but make sure no flour gets in between the layers.

2. Sprinkle a little flour on top of the dough. Use a dough scraper to tighten the surface of the dough by pushing the sides underneath the dough.

3. Use a dough scraper to chop the dough into two halves, if you wish to make two loaves. Lift the dough onto a baking sheet covered in nonstick baking paper by using your spatula and your other (flour-dusted) hand. Bake the bread as directed on pages 60–1, allowing about 30 minutes for two small loaves and 40–45 minutes for one large loaf.

HERITAGE WHEAT BAGUETTES

You can also make baguettes with your heritage wheat dough. Baguettes are small, so there will be a lot more crust than crumb, which will give extra crispiness and flavour. Bake the baguettes at a high temperature and perhaps for a little longer than you would usually do. You want the baguettes to have lots of colour, as this will give them a more interesting bite and a more distinct caramelized taste.

3 baguettes

YOUNG STARTER
see ingredients on page 63

DOUGH
see ingredients on page 63

YOUNG STARTER
Refresh your stock starter approximately 8 hours before use (see page 63).

DOUGH
See pages 55–60 for instructions on combining the ingredients, mixing the dough and leaving it to rise

Shape the dough once it has risen sufficiently by following steps 1 and 2 on page 63. Continue with the shaping instructions on page 66.

Bake the baguettes as specified on pages 60–1, for 20–25 minutes.

HOW TO SHAPE THE DOUGH INTO BAGUETTES

1. Use a dough scraper to cut the dough into three strips by placing the scraper about one-third of the way into the dough and cutting it. Then cut the remaining dough into two equal-sized strips.

2. Use a second dough scraper to scrape any leftover dough off the first scraper. Now tighten the surface of the dough by sprinkling a little flour onto the sides and pushing both sides of the dough underneath itself with the clean dough scraper.

3. Use the dough scraper and your (flour-dusted) hand to carefully lift the dough onto a baking sheet covered in nonstick baking paper.

4. Shape the remaining two baguettes in a similar manner and place them on the nonstick baking paper, leaving enough space between them to rise while baking.

HERITAGE WHEAT ROLLS

Heritage wheat dough can also be used to make rolls but they need to be baked at a high temperature and perhaps for a little longer than you would usually do. Longer baking will ensure they have lots of colour, a more interesting bite, and a more distinctly caramelized taste.

These rolls are fairly square and are supposed to look rustic, so don't overwork the dough or you'll risk knocking the air right out of it. They're great for breakfast, served on the side or even used to make sandwiches to go in your packed lunch.

12 rolls

YOUNG STARTER
see ingredients on page 63

DOUGH
see ingredients on page 63

YOUNG STARTER
Refresh your stock starter approximately 8 hours before use (see page 63).

DOUGH
See pages 55–60 for instructions on combining the ingredients, mixing the dough and leaving it to rise.

Shape the dough once it has risen sufficiently by following steps 1 and 2 on page 63. Then continue with the shaping instructions on page 70.

Bake the rolls following to the directions on pages 60–1, for 15–20 minutes.

HOW TO SHAPE THE DOUGH INTO ROLLS

1. Use a dough scraper to chop the dough in half lengthways.

2. Separate the halves into two sausage shapes, using the dough scraper, then tighten the surface of each one by pushing the sides underneath the dough.

3. Chop each 'sausage' into 6 square rolls.

4. Gently push the dough scraper underneath all the dough rolls.

5. Use the dough scraper and your other (flour-dusted) hand to carefully lift the rolls onto a baking sheet covered in nonstick baking paper. Place them 3–5 cm apart, to allow them enough space to rise while baking.

HERITAGE WHEAT LOAF

Baking heritage wheat bread in a loaf tin, as here, means you don't have to tighten the surface of the dough and shape it, so it might make baking the bread a little easier, too. While the look of your finished loaf will naturally be a little less rustic, you will still get a tender crumb and the lovely whole-grain aroma.

2 loaves, each baked in a tin
measuring 25 x 11 x 7 cm

YOUNG STARTER
see ingredients on page 63

DOUGH
see ingredients on page 63

YOUNG STARTER
Refresh your stock starter approximately 8 hours before use (see page 63).

DOUGH
Combine the ingredients and mix the dough as described on pages 55–9.

Grease the two tins thoroughly with butter, and ensure there are no bare spots.

Divide the mixed dough in two and pour into the baking tins. Press the dough down and place a piece of clingfilm loosely on top. Seal the edge with an elastic band to make sure the dough doesn't dry out.

Leave at room temperature for about one hour, then place in the fridge to rise for at least 12 hours, or until the dough has doubled in size. Check the dough a couple of hours before you want to bake the bread. If it hasn't risen sufficiently, remove the tins from the fridge to continue rising at room temperature. This step will awaken the yeast cells and enable them to complete the rise.

Preheat the oven to 250°C, Gas Mark 9; remove the clingfilm from the tins and place them in the oven. After 10 minutes, turn the temperature down to 230°C, Gas Mark 8, and bake until the loaves sound hollow when you tap the bases and their colour has turned a lovely dark brown – this will take a further 20–25 minutes. Turn the loaves out of the tins onto a rack to cool.

#USE A THERMOMETER
The first few times you bake bread in a tin, if you're not quite sure if your bread is done or not, we recommend that you check the loaf's internal temperature using a kitchen thermometer. Stick the probe straight into the middle of the bread. When the temperature is 98–100°C, the bread is ready to come out of the oven.

HERITAGE WHEAT BREAD BAKED IN A CASSEROLE

Try baking your heritage wheat bread in a lidded casserole. This will give you a beautifully round loaf that won't spread out in the oven. When you bake bread in a casserole, you also benefit from the steam that generates in the early stages of baking as condensation builds up inside. This will give your bread a lovely and slightly thicker crust than you'd get when baking free-form loaves.

You will need a large, solid flameproof casserole with a lid and a heavy base, such as a 4-litre cast iron casserole.

1 loaf

YOUNG STARTER
see ingredients on page 63

DOUGH
see ingredients on page 63

YOUNG STARTER
Refresh your stock starter approximately 8 hours before use (see page 63).

DOUGH
See pages 55–60 for instructions on combining the ingredients, mixing the dough, greasing the tin and leaving the dough to rise.

Turn your oven on to the highest possible temperature, and if it is a fan-assisted oven, turn that on as well. Place the casserole (covered with the lid) on the middle shelf to heat up.

Tighten the surface of the dough and shape it as described on page 63.

Wearing oven gloves, carefully take the now hot casserole out of the oven and place it on a pot holder or trivet. Remove the lid, and carefully transfer the dough to the casserole, seam-side up. Score the dough with a pair of sharp kitchen scissors. Cover with the hot lid (reminder: use oven gloves!) and return to the oven for 10 minutes. Reduce the heat to 230°C, Gas Mark 8. After 10 minutes, remove the lid and bake the bread for another 5 to 10 minutes. At this point, carefully remove the bread from the casserole. If it won't come out easily, let it bake for a little longer. When you're able to remove it, set the casserole aside but place the loaf of bread back inside directly on the shelf to finish baking. See page 61 for instructions on how to check if the bread is done.

HERITAGE WHEAT SNACK-BREAD

In our bakeries, we sell these little snack-breads made with basic Øland wheat dough and then stuffed with potatoes and cheese. Naturally, you can use different kinds of stuffing. They make a lovely snack and are perfect in your children's – or even your own – packed lunch.

The dough can be shaped and added to the foil tins and placed in the fridge the night before use. Then you can bake them in the morning before your kids leave for school.

8 small snack-breads, each baked in 12-cm diameter round foil baking tins

YOUNG STARTER
see ingredients on page 63

DOUGH
see ingredients on page 63

FILLING
300 g small potatoes, boiled, cooled, and cut into 1-cm dice
150 g North Sea Cheese (or a firm, hard cheese, such as Gouda), cut into 1-cm dice
small handful of lovage, wild garlic or fresh rosemary (optional)

YOUNG STARTER
Refresh your stock starter approximately 8 hours before use (see page 63).

DOUGH
See pages 55–60 for instructions on combining the ingredients, mixing the dough and leaving it to rise.

It's important that the oven is preheated to its highest possible temperature before baking the snack-breads.

Grease the foil baking tins with butter or oil. Shape the dough as described on page 63 and carefully chop into 8 pieces. Place the dough in the tins and gently press down. Then press pieces of potato and cheese into the dough, and scatter lovage on top. Leave at room temperature until the dough rises again. At this point you can refrigerate overnight and bake them the next day.

Bake the snack-breads as described on pages 60–1, for approximately 20 minutes.

#TIP
You can also bake the snack-breads in an ovenproof frying pan. Grease the tin with a little oil, if it's not nonstick. Place the dough in the tin, coat your fingers in a little oil and gently press down the dough. Press your filling into the dough, sprinkle with salt and drizzle with a little oil. Bake the snack-breads in the oven at 250°C, Gas Mark 9, for about 20 minutes.

HERITAGE WHEAT PIZZA

Heritage wheat dough can be used to make pizza with a wonderfully, supple crust with a hint of natural starter. Here, we have topped one of our pizzas with thinly sliced fennel bulbs, smoked cheese, lemon and edible nasturtium flowers, and thinly sliced smoked salmon and apples scattered with oxalis (wood sorrel) on the other, but you can use any kind of topping you like on these pizzas.

Makes 2 pizzas

YOUNG STARTER
see ingredients on page 63

DOUGH
see ingredients on page 63

TOPPING
150 g hard cheese such as Gouda, torn (or sliced)
any other toppings of your choice

YOUNG STARTER
Refresh your stock starter approximately 8 hours before use (see page 63).

DOUGH
See pages 55–60 for instructions on combining the ingredients, mixing the dough and leaving it to rise.

Before you are ready to bake, place a baking stone or pizza stone on the middle shelf of the oven. If you don't have a stone, you can get almost the same effect by using a baking sheet placed upside-down on the oven shelf. Turn the oven on to its highest possible setting.

The oven must have reached its highest temperature for at least 30 minutes before you bake the pizza.

Place a piece of nonstick baking paper on a flat, even surface, such as a pizza spade, the underside of a baking sheet, or the lid of a cardboard pizza box.

Carefully divide the risen dough in two and place one half on the nonstick baking paper. Dip your hands in water and flatten the dough until it covers the paper. Sprinkle the dough with half the cheese.

Open the oven door and quickly slide the paper with the pizza dough onto the hot baking stone or sheet, letting out as little heat as possible. Bake the pizza at the highest possible temperature, until the dough is golden and crisp and the cheese has melted and gained a little colour, for approximately 10 minutes. Bear in mind that baking times can vary greatly, depending on how hot your oven is, so keep an eye on it.

Remove the pizza from the oven and bake the other as described above. Spread the toppings onto the pizzas and serve.

SEEDED BREAD

In this recipe we've added pumpkin seeds as well as whole boiled wheat berries to the basic dough. These ingredients impart a little liveliness to the bread as well as a different bite and texture. Wheat berries also give the bread a lovely flavour similar to popcorn. Choose your favourite whole-grain wheat flour or use whatever's in your cupboard.

1 large loaf or 2 small ones

YOUNG STARTER
50 g wheat stock starter
100 g water
30 g bread flour
30 g whole-grain flour

DOUGH
550 g cold water
50 g young starter
5 g fresh organic baking yeast
150 g whole-grain wheat flour
450 g bread flour
15 g salt
wheat flakes, for sprinkling

BERRIES AND SEEDS
75 g wheat berries
75 g pumpkin seeds

TOPPING
wheat flakes

YOUNG STARTER
Refresh your stock starter approximately 8 hours before use (see page 63).

BERRIES
Boil the wheat berries in lightly salted water for 40 minutes. Drain and leave to cool completely before adding them to the dough.

DOUGH
Combine the ingredients (minus the wheat berries and seeds) and mix the dough as described on pages 55–9. Then carefully add the cooled berries and the seeds and mix gently until evenly distributed. If you're using a food stand mixer, this should take about 10 seconds on the lowest speed.

Let the dough rise and then shape it as described on page 60.

Sprinkle with wheat flakes and bake as described on pages 60–1, for approximately 40 minutes for one large loaf or 30 minutes for two small loaves.

#TIP
Boil the wheat berries well ahead, for example, at the same time you refresh your stock starter. Then they'll be cool and ready for use when you need them.

#TIP
You can also use this dough to make rolls by following the instructions for the heritage wheat rolls on page 68.

FINE WHEAT BREAD

This bread is made solely with plain bread flour and contains no whole-grain flour. This gives the bread a very open crumb and, because the dough contains a natural starter and has a substantially long rising time, you'll still get a lovely characteristic flavour. Spoil yourself and your family from time to time with this luxurious loaf.

1 large loaf or 2 small ones

YOUNG STARTER
see ingredients on page 63

DOUGH
550 g cold water
50 g young starter
5 g fresh organic baking yeast
600 g bread flour
15 g salt

YOUNG STARTER
Refresh your stock starter approximately 8 hours before use (see page 63).

DOUGH
Combine the ingredients, mix the dough, leave it to rise and shape it following the instructions on pages 55–60.

Bake following the instructions on pages 60–1, for approximately 40–45 minutes for one large loaf or 30 minutes for two small loaves.

HERITAGE WHEAT BREAD WITH STONE-MILLED HERITAGE WHEAT

You can make this bread entirely with stone-milled heritage bread flour, such as emmer or spelt or one of the rural sorts. When flour is stone-milled, parts of both the bran and germ will be left in the flour, adding flavour as well as vitamins. This means you'll get a really nutritious loaf of bread with a very pure taste of heritage wheat.

1 large loaf or 2 small ones

YOUNG STARTER
see ingredients on page 63

DOUGH
550 g cold water
50 g young starter
5 g fresh organic baking yeast
600 g heritage bread flour
15 g salt

YOUNG STARTER
Refresh your stock starter approximately 8 hours before use (see page 63).

DOUGH
Combine the ingredients, mix the dough, leave it to rise and shape it following the instructions on pages 55–60.

Bake following the instructions on pages 60–1, for approximately 40–45 minutes for one large loaf or 30 minutes for two small loaves.

WHEAT BREAD WITHOUT A STARTER

You can still bake delicious wheat bread without using a natural starter, but it won't be quite as aromatic as when you do. However, if you let the dough rise for a long time, you'll get a loaf of bread that's almost as tasty, and with a delicate and moist crumb.

While dough made with a starter needs to be baked within 24 hours of mixing, dough made without a starter offers more flexibility time-wise. In fact, letting the dough rise for more than 24 hours gives the flavours more time to develop, resulting in even better bread. In the fridge, the dough will continue to develop flavour for up to three days, though we find that the dough peaks after about 48 hours.

This dough comes in handy because you can make big portions of dough, then bake it in smaller portions after rising for one, two and three days, respectively.

1 large loaf or 2 small ones

DOUGH
550 g cold water
5 g fresh organic baking yeast
150 g whole-grain wheat flour
450 g bread flour
15 g salt

DOUGH
Combine the ingredients, mix the dough, leave it to rise and shape it as described on pages 55–60. Please note that you can let this dough rise for a minimum 12 hours, but the finished bread will be much better if the dough is left to rise in the fridge for 24–48 hours.

Bake following the instructions on pages 60–1, for approximately 40–45 minutes for one large loaf or 30 minutes for two small loaves.

RYE AND WHEAT BREAD

In our rye and wheat bread, the wheat flour imparts lightness while the rye flour imparts depth and density. This recipe makes the classic kind of rustic French pain de campagne you would normally only find at open-air markets in France, next to the cans of rabbit pâté and confit de canard, and jars of fig preserve. It's wonderfully filling, and has become a Meyer's Bakery classic.

1 large loaf or 2 small ones

YOUNG STARTER
see ingredients on page 63

DOUGH
550 g cold water
50 g young starter
5 g fresh organic baking yeast
150 g rye flour
450 g bread flour
15 g salt

YOUNG STARTER
Refresh your stock starter approximately 8 hours before use (see page 63).

DOUGH
Combine the ingredients and mix the dough following the instructions on pages 55–9.

Please note that if you mix the rye-wheat dough in a food stand mixer, you have to be careful, because the gluten quality in rye is not the same as in wheat. This makes the dough more vulnerable to over-mixing, so don't mix it at the highest speed and keep a constant eye on the dough after the first 5 minutes of mixing. The dough is finished as soon as it slips off the sides of the bowl. If you continue to mix the dough, it risks losing its elasticity, which will give you a much denser crumb.

Let the dough rise and then shape it as described on page 60.

Bake following the instructions on pages 60–1, for approximately 40–45 minutes for one large loaf or 30 minutes for two small loaves.

PURPLE WHEAT BERRY BREAD WITH WALNUTS AND CRANBERRIES

Purple wheat berries are very aromatic and bring unique characteristics to baked goods. The bran contains high levels of anthocyanin, a red-purple dye that imparts both dough and finished bread with a purple hue and a distinctive flavour. Anthocyanin, which is considered to be an antioxidant, is also found in red cabbage and blackberries.

In this recipe, the walnuts and cranberries add extra flavour, crunchiness and texture. You can also add cranberry juice if you like, to boost the colour of the finished loaf.

1 large loaf or 2 small ones

YOUNG STARTER
see ingredients on page 63

DOUGH
550 g cold water
50 g young starter
2 teaspoons cranberry juice (optional)
5 g fresh organic baking yeast
500 g bread flour
100 g whole-grain purple wheat berry flour
15 g salt
40 g walnuts, coarsely chopped
40 g dried cranberries

TOPPING
poppy seeds

YOUNG STARTER
Refresh your stock starter approximately 8 hours before use (see page 63).

DOUGH
Combine all the ingredients except the walnuts and dried cranberries, and mix the dough following the instructions on pages 55–9.

Add the walnuts and cranberries and mix gently until evenly distributed. If you are using a food stand mixer, this should only take 10 seconds on the lowest speed.

Let the dough rise and then shape it as described on page 60.

Sprinkle with poppy seeds and bake following the instructions on pages 60–1, for approximately 40–45 minutes for one large loaf or 30 minutes for two small loaves.

DALAR WHEAT BREAD WITH SEEDS

Dalar is a type of Scandinavian heritage wheat with a distinct sweetness and intense flavour. As the name indicates, it comes from Dalarna, in Sweden. In this recipe from Meyer's Bakeries we use both berries and whole-grain flour. The high protein and gluten content produce extremely expansive dough, which results in a loaf that stays moist for a long time. If you cannot get Dalar, any other heritage wheat variety will work.

1 large loaf or 2 small ones

YOUNG STARTER
see ingredients on page 63

BERRIES & SEEDS
100 g cracked Dalar heritage wheat
 berries (or regular wheat berries)
70 g pumpkin seeds

DOUGH
550 g cold water
50 g young starter
5 g fresh organic baking yeast
500 g bread flour
100 g Dalar or other whole-grain
 heritage wheat flour
18 g salt
1 teaspoon dark malt syrup

TOPPING
rolled oats (optional)

YOUNG STARTER
Refresh your stock starter approximately 8 hours before use (see page 63).

BERRIES & SEEDS
Soak the cracked wheat berries in cold water overnight. Drain the berries thoroughly before adding them to the dough.

DOUGH
Combine all the ingredients except the soaked berries and pumpkin seeds, and mix the dough as described on pages 55–9.

Add the soaked wheat berries and the pumpkin seeds and mix gently until evenly distributed. If you are using a food stand mixer, this should only take 10 seconds on the lowest speed.

Let the dough rise and then shape it as described on page 60.

Sprinkle with rolled wheat, if using, the bake following the instructions on pages 60–1, for approximately 50 minutes for one large loaf or 30 minutes for two small loaves.

#TIP
You can also use whole berries in this dough. Boil the berries for 40 minutes in lightly salted water, drain thoroughly and leave to cool before adding them to the dough.

OAT BREAD WITH PORRIDGE AND ROLLED OATS

You get a triple helping of oats in this recipe. We use oat flour and porridge in the dough and then sprinkle the loaf with rolled oats. The oat flour imparts a delicate yet hearty sweetness to the bread, while the porridge gives it a lovely moist crumb and that wonderful taste of oats. The rolled oats add texture and a decorative finish. Bake this bread when you have leftover porridge – or make a large portion on purpose.

1 large loaf or 2 small ones

YOUNG STARTER
50 g stock starter
100 g water
30 g bread flour
30 g whole-grain wheat flour

PORRIDGE
50 g finely rolled oat flakes
150 g water
a pinch of salt

DOUGH
300 g cold water
50 g young starter
5 g fresh organic baking yeast
150 g whole-grain oat flour
450 g bread flour
15 g salt
200 g porridge oats

TOPPING
rolled oats

YOUNG STARTER
Refresh your stock starter approximately 8 hours before use (see page 63).

PORRIDGE
Bring the rolled oats, water and salt to the boil then reduce the heat to low and cook for approximately 2 minutes then remove from the heat and leave to cool.

DOUGH
Combine all the ingredients, except the porridge and coarsely rolled oats, and mix the dough as described on pages 55–9. Add the cold porridge to the dough and mix gently until evenly distributed. If you are using a stand mixer, this should only take 10 seconds on the lowest speed.

Let the dough rise and then shape it as described on page 60.

Sprinkle the loaf with the rolled oats and bake, following the instructions on pages 60–1, for approximately 40 to 45 minutes for one large loaf or 30 minutes for two small loaves.

WHAT'S WRONG WITH MY WHEAT BREAD – AND HOW DO I FIX IT?

Things don't always go according to plan when you bake bread with high hydration wheat dough, or any other dough included in this book, for that matter. Of course, it's frustrating, but it happens to most people. Even the best bakers around make mistakes from time to time. It's all about minimizing the number of mistakes you make and increasing the number of successes, and you can only do this by learning from your previous mistakes.

Below you'll find a guide to some of the most common problems you might come across. We'll provide you with examples of what might be wrong, advice on what you should be aware of the next time around and tips about what you can do if you notice that something's wrong along the way.

Please note that there may be several reasons for the same problem and sometimes there might even be directly opposing reasons behind the same issue. When this happens, you may have to consider which reason is most likely to have caused your specific problem or perhaps try to correct several different things at once.

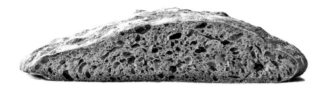

MY LOAF IS FLAT

Your dough has not been mixed sufficiently, which means that the gluten strands aren't strong enough to hold the dough together

Mix your dough for a little longer and conduct the gluten test (see page 281) to make sure you've mixed the dough sufficiently before you leave it to rise.

Your dough has been over-mixed, which has made the gluten strands weak; the structure of the dough has been compromised

This only happens when you use a food stand mixer to mix your dough. Next time, stop the mixer as soon as the dough gathers around the dough hook and slips off the insides of the bowl. (You can read more about gluten strands on page 280.)

Your dough has been left to rise for too long before going into the oven

Leaving the dough rise for too long means there's not enough texture or support left in it, so it collapses and spreads (a little like a soufflé). Even though it's important that dough is given time to rise properly prior to baking, there must be some rising power left in the dough to enable it to rise a little inside the oven during baking. Next time, let the dough rise for a slightly shorter period of time, or it let it rise in a slightly cooler place.

If you sense that your dough is over-risen, you can knock the air out of the dough by punching it down and then placing it in two greased baking tins, just to be on the safe side. Leave the dough to rise at room temperature and then bake as described in the Heritage Wheat Loaf recipe, which is baked in a tin, on page 73.

Your oven was not hot enough when you put the bread dough in it

If your oven wasn't preheated for long enough, the dough won't get the heat-shock it needs and it will slowly spread instead of rising. At least 30 minutes before baking, place a baking stone or upside-down baking sheet in the oven on the middle shelf and turn the heat up to the highest temperature. Once you have slid the loaf onto the baking stone or baking sheet shut the oven door as quickly as you can to stop the heat escaping.

MY BREAD CRUMB IS TOO DENSE

Your dough has not risen sufficiently

Make sure your dough rises to almost double in size before carefully tipping it out of its bowl or container.

You have worked your dough too hard, possibly knocking the air out of it as you chopped and tightened the surface of it

Be very careful as you tip your dough out of the bowl or container after rising. If it's difficult to get the dough out, next time try greasing the container or bowl with oil before placing the dough in it. Also, make sure you handle your dough with care as you chop it into smaller portions, tighten the surface of it and slide it onto the nonstick baking paper. Work the dough as gently as possible to avoid knocking the air out of it.

When you handle dough that doesn't appear to behave in the way you were expecting, to be on the safe side, place it in two greased baking tins. Leave the dough to rise at room temperature and then bake as described in the Heritage Wheat Loaf recipe on page 73.

Your dough has over-risen

If you've left the dough to rise for too long its structure will have become porous and the dough will tend to collapse a little as you chop it into smaller portions or when you slide it into the oven. Next time try leaving the dough to rise for a shorter period of time.

If you notice the dough is rising more than it should, you can always punch it back and leave it to rise again, but keep an eye on the time you leave it to rise (see page 60).

You haven't mixed your dough enough

Mix it some more (see page 280). Further mixing will strengthen the gluten strands and enable them to hold on to the carbon dioxide generated by the yeast cells, which will leave bigger holes in the crumb. If you're in doubt as to whether or not your dough needs more mixing, perform the gluten test as described on page 281, before leaving the dough to rise.

The protein content in your flour is too low

Try using flour that contains at least 12 per cent protein, which will ensure stronger gluten strands and a lighter crumb.

There is too much whole-grain flour in your dough

The more whole-grain flour you use, the denser your crumb. If you want a more open crumb, try using a little less whole-grain flour.

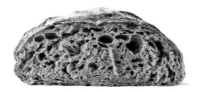 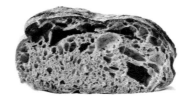

MY CRUMB IS 'DOUGHY'

Your bread is not entirely baked so the crumb is very wet and sticky
Check the temperature of the bread using a kitchen thermometer next time you bake to ensure the centre of the bread has reached 98°C, at which point the bread will be done.

Your dough has not risen sufficiently
Leave the dough to rise for a little longer next time you bake. If you notice that dough left in the fridge is not rising as much as it should, place it somewhere warm to stimulate the yeast cells into action.

THERE ARE HOLES UNDERNEATH THE CRUST AND A DENSE CRUMB AT THE BOTTOM OF THE BREAD

Your dough has been left to rise for too long (in the fridge)
This will make the crust settle quickly after placing the dough in the oven, as the dough immediately beneath the crust will be too porous and drop to the bottom part of the bread during baking. Next time, leave the dough to rise for a shorter period of time to make it less porous and to leave it with a little power to rise that final bit once it's in the oven.

High oven temperature combined with dough that's too cold
Leave the dough at room temperature in its container for a short while before tipping it out onto the work surface to avoid baking dough that's too cold.

Your dough has not risen sufficiently before going into the oven
Insufficient rising time will cause the top to react to the heat-shock and rise quickly. Leave the dough to rise a little longer next time you bake.

MY BREAD IS TOO SOUR

Your dough has been left to rise for too long
Reduce the rising time next time you bake.

Your young starter has been left for too long which has made it sour
Leave the young starter at room temperature for a short while before mixing it into the dough. If the young starter smells and tastes too sour to add to the dough, add a little less to stop your finished bread tasting too sour.

Your bread is not done
Bread may turn sour if it isn't quite done by the time it is taken out of the oven. Insert a kitchen thermometer into the centre of the loaf and check that the bread has reached 98–100°C before removing it from the oven.

WHOLE-GRAIN BREADS

Bread made with freshly milled
whole-grain flour is delightfully rustic,
with a tender, open crumb, a dark brown
crust and a profound sweetness.

WHOLE-GRAIN BREADS

Whole-grain flour contains all of the grain's bran and germ. Eating whole-grain bread means you will enjoy all the lovely aromas as well as benefit from the grains' entire package of fat, fibres, minerals, vitamins and antioxidants. And, of course, the most satisfactory and pleasurable way of ensuring you consume whole grains on a daily basis is by baking your own whole-grain bread.

Long-rise bread with plenty of whole-grain flour has a wonderfully hearty taste; it's not only filling but it's healthy, too. Baking our inspiring recipes will enable you and your family to get the daily recommended fibre intake that will help stave off lifestyle-related illnesses, including coronary thrombosis, cancer, diabetes and obesity. And eating enough fibre also helps stabilize your blood sugar throughout the day.

Working with dough that contains a high level of whole-grain flour is different from working with the various types of wheat dough we taught you to handle in the previous chapter. This is partly because whole-grain flour (relatively speaking) contains less gluten than sifted flour, as it contains both bran and germ, while the sifted flour we use only contains endosperm (the part of the grain that contains gluten).

Furthermore, bran and germ 'slice' gluten structures, which is why you have to pay extra attention when mixing your whole-grain dough, or it may not rise properly.

The coarser the flour, the wetter the dough must be as you mix it in order to yield a tender rather than a dry crumb. Wet dough also has a tendency to spread, which is why I bake all my whole-grain breads in loaf tins.

Granted, whole-grain bread will never have a crumb as open as that of bread baked with bread flour. On the other hand, nothing beats the delicious and hearty grain aroma you get with freshly milled whole-grain flour.

We love baking with whole-grain flours such as einkorn, emmer, spelt, barley and all the other types of ancient and rural wheat found in the recipes in this chapter. Each and every one of

these different types of flour yields sublimely tender and tasty breads with a fantastic, crystal-splintering crisp crust.

On the following pages, we'll provide you with a basic recipe for whole-grain bread made with 100 per cent whole-grain flour and virtually equal quantities of water and flour, a little natural starter and a smidgen of baking yeast, as well as honey and salt. Mix, and pour the dough into a loaf tin, then leave to rise and bake. It's that simple. And once you get the hang of the basic recipe, you can move on to explore the other recipes where we use 75 per cent or 50 per cent whole-grain flour supplemented with other types of flour as well as seeds, berries, herbs, vegetables and fruit.

STARTER

When you use a lot of whole-grain flour to bake bread, you should use both a natural starter and yeast. The starter only provides limited rising power, but its primary task is to impart a lovely flavour and an extendable crumb, ensuring your bread stays fresh for longer. If you don't already have a batch of natural starter, see page 39 for information on how to get hold of one or make your own.

REFRESH YOUR STARTER

A starter needs to be refreshed 8–12 hours before being used to make whole-grain dough in order to ensure that the starter is active as well as mild and elegant in taste. Remove the stock starter from the fridge or wherever you are storing it and add flour and water (see page 40). This will turn it into young starter, which you then leave at room temperature. Feel free to use the same type of flour that you'll be using for your bread. The starter is ready to use when its surface starts bubbling. It should also taste a little like a sour dairy product and smell like freshly brewed beer or champagne.

#EMERGENCY SOLUTION

In an emergency, if you haven't had time (or have simply forgotten) to refresh your starter before baking, you can add 1 tablespoon of wheat stock starter or 1 teaspoon of stock rye starter directly to the dough. You won't get the same impact in terms of taste and texture, but the unrefreshed starter will still add some character to your bread.

INGREDIENTS

Mixing dough made with whole-grain flour is much like mixing dough made with bread flour, but you will notice that the flour behaves differently.

FLOUR

Whole-grain flour is a high-extraction type of flour, where 100 per cent of the bran and germ remain in the flour (you can read more about extraction on page 34). Dough with a high content of stone-milled whole-grain flour doesn't rise as easily as dough made with plain flour or bread flour for two reasons. First, the bran and germ in the whole-grain flour have absolutely no rising power whatsoever and, second, the flour particles are coarser than those found in regular flour. However, the bran and germ contain lots of vitamins and minerals, which make whole-grain flour more nutritious.

#USE FRESHLY MILLED WHOLE-GRAIN FLOUR

Regardless of the type of whole-grain flour you choose to bake with, always make sure it's freshly milled. As soon as the flour is milled, the fat contained in the germ and bran starts to become rancid, which will eventually impart the flour with a bitter taste. Preferably, whole-grain flour should be no more than one month old, so look closely at the best-before date when you buy whole-grain flour. The fresher the flour, the tastier your bread.

In our bakeries, we mill our own whole-grain flour on a daily basis and we also sell freshly milled whole-grain flour. But you can also mill your own whole-grain flour, either at home on a small electric mill (see page 16) or in shops with mills for public use. That way you'll never be short of freshly milled, aromatic flour.

WATER

The high content of fibre in the whole-grain bran and germ enables whole-grain flour to absorb more than 100 per cent of its own weight, which is much more water than regular wheat flour can. The ability to absorb more water yields bread with an incredibly tender crumb.

YEAST

We bake all of our whole-grain breads with a smidgen of baking yeast and a little natural starter. The tiny amount of baking yeast enables the dough to rise sufficiently without the finished loaf tasting too strongly of yeast. We recommend that you use organic yeast because it contains more yeast strains than conventional yeast, which adds more flavour to your bread. (Read more about yeast on page 282.)

SALT

Salt strengthens the somewhat fragile gluten strands in whole-grain flour and therefore improves the crumb. We use regular fine salt, but you can also use fine sea salt or Himalayan salt that's been milled. The latter takes a little longer to dissolve, but it contains more minerals and has a more pronounced taste.

HONEY

Whole-grain bran and germ taste a little bitter, and this needs to be balanced with some sweetness. You can use regular sugar, but we use honey because, as well as sweetening the bread, it adds flavour and character.

COMBINE THE INGREDIENTS AND MIX THE DOUGH

Whole-grain flour is coarse, so you'll have to mix your dough for a bit longer before it becomes sufficiently smooth and expandable. The presence of bran and germ delay the construction of gluten strands as you mix the dough, which is why whole-grain dough won't come together as quickly as dough made with regular bread flour or plain flour. This is where your food stand mixer will come in really handy. Naturally, you can also mix this dough by hand, but you need a lot of muscle as well as time and patience (see Three Mixing Methods on pages 55–59). If you don't have a food mixer you can also autolyse the dough to kick-start the mixing (see page 278).

HOW TO MIX WHOLE-GRAIN DOUGH

1. Mix the cold water and natural starter in the mixing bowl of a stand mixer. Sprinkle in the yeast and stir until it dissolves.

2. Add the flour and salt.

3. Attach the dough hook and set the mixer to its lowest setting for approximately 1 minute. This will gather the ingredients and stop the flour flying everywhere.

4. Increase the speed and mix the dough thoroughly. The mixing time will vary depending on the water-to-flour ratio. Keep an eye on the dough. At the exact moment it comes away from the inside of the bowl and starts to cling to the dough hook, turn the stand mixer off immediately because the dough is ready.

5. For added reassurance, you can do the gluten test (see page 281) to make sure that the dough is thoroughly mixed.

POUR THE DOUGH INTO A LOAF TIN TO RISE

Once you've finished mixing the dough, it needs to rise by 50 per cent before baking. It contains a lot of water, so whole-grain dough is very soft. For this reason, we bake our whole-grain breads in tins measuring 25 x 12 x 7 cm.

Grease the loaf tin well with butter. Fill it only halfway up with dough to leave enough room for the dough to rise. Place a piece of clingfilm over the top and secure it with an elastic band around the edge of the tin to stop the dough drying out. Leave at room temperature for approximately 1 to 2 hours to ensure the yeast is alive and kicking before placing it in the fridge, where the dough should rise by 50 per cent. This will take at least 12 hours. Check the dough a couple of hours before you want to bake your bread. If the dough hasn't risen sufficiently, remove the tin from the fridge and leave in a warm place for a few hours. This will 'awaken' the yeast cells and enable the dough to finish rising.

#TIP

If you line the tin with nonstick baking paper, it'll be easier to get the bread out without breaking it. Grease the tin first with a little butter and then line the tin with the paper. This way, the butter helps the paper stick to the inside of the tin.

BAKING YOUR BREAD

When baking using a loaf tin, the same principles apply as when you bake free-form loaves, but with a few extra rules.

Take the loaf tin out of the fridge 1 hour before you want to bake, then turn your oven on to its highest temperature at least half an hour before baking. Use the fan-assisted function if your oven has it, and keep it on while baking. Remove the clingfilm from the loaf tin and place the tin on the middle shelf of the oven. Bake at full heat for the first 5 minutes, then turn the heat down to 200°C, Gas Mark 6. Leave the bread to bake at this temperature until it is done. Ovens differ in terms of how hot they get and the way they distribute heat, so all baking times we give here are approximations. Keep an eye on your bread while it bakes. When it turns beautifully dark and sounds hollow when you tap it, you will know it is done. You can also use a kitchen thermometer to check the core temperature. When it reaches 98–100°C, the bread is done.

Tip the bread out of the loaf tin and place it on a cooling rack. Allowing air to circulate all around the freshly baked loaf stops it accumulating condensation, and will save your bread from having a boring, soft crust.

#TIP

Use a thermometer the first few times you bake whole-grain bread, until you feel comfortable with your oven and have a sense of how hot it will get and how long you should bake your bread.

STORING WHOLE-GRAIN BREAD

The best way to store whole-grain bread is at room temperature, wrapped in nonstick baking paper. This will allow the bread to breathe and keep the crust crisp. If you don't expect to eat all of your bread in the next day or two, seal the portion you want to last longer in a resealable plastic food bag and keep it in the fridge. Then, when you want to eat your bread, you can heat it in a preheated oven at 200°C, Gas Mark 6, or slice it and toast it in a toaster This will make it nice and tender again (you can even rub a little water into the bread before heating it to re-establish a sense of freshly baked bread).

100 PER CENT WHOLE-GRAIN BREAD

In our basic whole-grain bread recipe, we use only whole-grain wheat flour with all of its bran and germ as this gives you the pure and profound grain flavour along with all the nutrients, vitamins and minerals contained in the flour. This bread is a bit like a cross between a light rye bread and a tender heritage wheat bread.

1 loaf of bread, baked in a tin measuring
25 x 12 x 7 cm

YOUNG STARTER
50 g stock starter
100 g water
60 g whole-grain wheat flour

DOUGH
450 g water
50 g young starter
5 g fresh organic baking yeast
10 g honey
500 g whole-grain wheat flour
10 g salt

YOUNG STARTER
Refresh your stock starter 8–12 hours before use (see page 40). Whisk all the ingredients in a small bowl with a removable lid and leave at room temperature. The portion of young starter you don't use in the dough will now become your stock starter for future use (see diagram on page 39).

DOUGH
Combine the ingredients and mix the dough as described on pages 108–9.

Pour the dough into the greased loaf tin and leave to rise for at least 12 hours as described on page 110.

Bake the bread following the instructions on page 110, for approximately 40–45 minutes.

75 PER CENT WHOLE-GRAIN BREAD

In this recipe, we use 75 per cent whole-grain wheat flour, which includes most of the flour's valuable properties but yields dough that is a little easier to work with than 100 per cent whole-grain dough. People who prefer a golden crust should try this recipe!

1 loaf of bread, baked in a tin measuring 25 x 12 x 7 cm

YOUNG STARTER
see ingredients on page 113

DOUGH
450 g water
50 g young starter
5 g fresh organic baking yeast
10 g honey
375 g whole-grain wheat flour
125 g bread flour
10 g salt

YOUNG STARTER
Refresh your stock starter 8–12 hours before use (see page 113).

DOUGH
Combine the ingredients and mix the dough as described on pages 108–9.

Pour the dough into the greased loaf tin and leave to rise for at least 12 hours as described on page 110.

Bake the bread following the instructions on page 110, for approximately 40–45 minutes.

50 PER CENT WHOLE-GRAIN BREAD

Removing some of the bran and germ that weaken the gluten strands will yield dough that rises effortlessly and produce a loaf of bread with a more open crumb. In this recipe, we've exchanged half the amount of whole-grain wheat flour with regular wheat flour. Because 50 per cent of the flour is still whole-grain, however, the finished loaf is considered to be whole-grain bread. We use this dough with seeds, berries and other kinds of added extras as well.

1 loaf of bread, baked in a tin measuring 25 x 12 x 7 cm

YOUNG STARTER
see ingredients on page 113

DOUGH
450 g water
50 g young starter
5 g fresh organic baking yeast
10 g honey
250 g whole-grain wheat flour
250 g bread flour
10 g salt

YOUNG STARTER
Refresh your stock starter 8–12 hours before use (see page 113).

DOUGH
Combine the ingredients and mix the dough as described on pages 108–9.

Pour the dough into the greased loaf tin and leave to rise for at least 12 hours as described on page 110.

Bake the bread following the instructions on page 110, for approximately 40–45 minutes.

GRANOLA BARS WITH RAISINS AND HAZELNUTS

At Meyer's Bakeries we try to help combat food waste. One of the ways we do this is to use any leftover whole-grain dough to make our Granola Bars. We sweeten the dough with treacle syrup, a residual product from the industrial production of sugar from sugar canes and sugar beets. (You can use molasses if you cannot get treacle syrup.) In this recipe we use our 50 per cent whole-grain dough, adding raisins and nuts for extra bite and crunchiness. You will also need 12 mini loaf tins or a large muffin tin. Be sure to grease them well before adding the dough.

12 mini bars

YOUNG STARTER
see ingredients on page 113

DOUGH
see ingredients on page 117

FILLING
150 g raisins
150 g hazelnuts
20 g treacle syrup (or molasses)

TOPPING
wheat flakes

YOUNG STARTER
Refresh your stock starter 8–12 hours before use (see page 113).

DOUGH
Combine all the ingredients, except the filling, and mix the dough as described on pages 108–9. Once you've finished mixing the dough, add the raisins, hazelnuts and treacle (or molasses) and gently mix them in. This should take 1–2 minutes in a food stand mixer with the motor on low speed.

Pour the dough into the greased mini loaf tins or muffin tin and leave to rise for at least 12 hours as described on page 110.

Sprinkle with wheat flakes and bake following the instructions on page 110, for approximately 25 minutes. Transfer to a rack to cool.

#TIP
If you have some leftover dough from any other type of bread, add one-third of the filling and make Granola Bars out of that.

#TIP
To transfer all of the tins in and out of the oven quickly and easily, arrange them on one or two large preheated baking trays.

CHARGRILLED WHOLE-GRAIN BREAD WITH POTATOES AND BACON

In this recipe, we add bacon and potatoes to our 50 per cent whole-grain wheat dough, which makes an excellent snack-bread. You can add different fillings practically ad infinitum. Eat on its own as a snack or serve with soup or stew or chargrilled and spread with smoked cheese and salad, as here.

1 loaf of bread, baked in a tin measuring
25 x 12 x 7 cm

YOUNG STARTER
see ingredients on page 113

DOUGH
see ingredients on page 117

FILLING
**150 g peeled potatoes, boiled, cooled
and diced**
**60 g bacon, fried cooled and broken
into smaller pieces**

EXTRAS
**neutral oil or melted butter (for brushing
the bread)**
smoked cheese
mixed green salad with lots of fresh herbs

YOUNG STARTER
Refresh your stock starter 8–12 hours before use (see page 113).

DOUGH
Combine all the ingredients, except the filling, and mix the dough as described on pages 108–9. When you've finished mixing the dough, add the diced potatoes and bacon and mix until evenly distributed. This will take 1 to 2 minutes in a food stand mixer on low speed.

Pour the dough into the greased loaf tin and let rise as described on page 110.

Bake the bread following the instructions on page 110, for approximately 40–45 minutes.

Tip the bread out of the tin and onto a rack to cool. Slice and brush with a little neutral oil or melted butter. Place on a grill pan over a high heat and chargrill the slices of bread. To serve, spread the hot slices of bread with smoked cheese and place a small handful of green salad on top.

WHOLE-GRAIN BREAD WITH APPLES AND SUNFLOWER SEEDS

Whole-grain dough can be varied endlessly. Grated apples and sunflower seeds impart this recipe with a sweet and sour flavour, as well as a tender yet crunchy crumb. You can also use grated carrots, squash or any other vegetable lurking in your fridge.

1 loaf of bread, baked in a tin measuring
25 x 12 x 7 cm

YOUNG STARTER
see ingredients on page 113

DOUGH
see ingredients on page 117

FILLING
2 apples, grated and juice squeezed out, or
100 g some other grated vegetable
of your choice
75 g sunflower seeds

YOUNG STARTER
Refresh your stock starter 8–12 hours before use (see page 113).

DOUGH
Combine all the ingredients, except the filling, and mix the dough as described on pages 108–9. When you've finished mixing the dough, add the grated apples and sunflower seeds and mix until evenly distributed. This will take 1–2 minutes in a food stand mixer on low speed.

Pour the dough into the greased baking tin and leave to rise as described on page 110 for at least 12 hours.

Bake the bread following the instructions on page 110, for approximately 40–45 minutes.

#TIP
You can use the apple juice squeezed from the apples in your dough instead of an equivalent amount of water. Just make sure you add 450 g in all.

100 PER CENT SPELT BREAD

Compared with regular wheat, spelt, which is the best-known heritage wheat, has a full and very pronounced flavour. The gluten strands in spelt are not as strong as those in wheat so, in order to get bread with an open crumb, spelt dough requires more careful mixing.

1 loaf of bread, baked in a tin measuring 25 x 12 x 7 cm

YOUNG STARTER
see ingredients on page 113

DOUGH
450 g water
50 g young starter
5 g fresh organic baking yeast
10 g honey
250 g whole-grain spelt flour
250 g sifted spelt flour
10 g salt

YOUNG STARTER
Refresh your stock starter 8–12 hours before use (see page 113).

DOUGH
Combine all the ingredients and mix the dough as described on pages 108–9.

Pour the dough into the greased baking tin and leave to rise for at least 12 hours as described on page 110.

Bake the bread following the instructions on page 110, for approximately 40–45 minutes.

EMMER BREAD

Emmer is possibly my favourite heritage wheat. Much like spelt, the gluten strands in emmer aren't terribly strong, which is why we add regular wheat flour to this dough to make it rise. The emmer bread is quite dark and succulent and has a fantastic, very distinctive flavour.

1 loaf of bread, baked in a tin measuring 25 x 12 x 7 cm

YOUNG STARTER
see ingredients on page 113

DOUGH
450 g water
50 g young starter
5 g fresh organic baking yeast
10 g honey
250 g whole-grain emmer flour
250 g bread flour
10 g salt

YOUNG STARTER
Refresh your stock starter 8–12 hours before use (see page 113).

DOUGH
Combine all the ingredients and mix the dough as described on pages 108–9.

Pour the dough into the greased baking tin and leave to rise for at least 12 hours as described on page 110.

Bake the bread following the instructions on page 110, for approximately 40–45 minutes.

EINKORN BREAD

Einkorn is the oldest type of heritage wheat, and the bread it yields is beautifully golden-yellow with a wonderfully strong and delicious grain flavour. Much like spelt and emmer the gluten strands in einkorn aren't terribly strong, which is why we add regular wheat flour to this dough to make it rise.

1 loaf of bread, baked in a tin measuring 25 x 12 x 7 cm

YOUNG STARTER
see ingredients on page 113

DOUGH
450 g water
50 g young starter
5 g fresh organic baking yeast
10 g honey
250 g whole-grain einkorn flour
250 g bread flour
10 g salt

YOUNG STARTER
Refresh your stock starter 8–12 hours before use (see page 113).

DOUGH
Combine all the ingredients together and mix the dough as described on pages 108–9.

Pour the dough into the greased baking tin and leave to rise for at least 12 hours as described on page 110.

Bake the bread following the instructions on page 110, for approximately 40–45 minutes.

BARLEY BREAD

It can be tricky to bake only with barley flour, but it has such a lovely flavour and contains more essential and cholesterol-reducing amino acids than wheat or rye flour. At Meyer's Bakeries, after a lot of experimentation, we found that using 50 per cent barley flour and 50 per cent bread flour gives us a loaf that's somewhere between whole-grain wheat bread and rye bread. The bread flour provides the dough with strong gluten strands that enable it to rise. Barley flour is a little bitter, but we balance this with honey.

1 loaf of bread, baked in a tin measuring 25 x 12 x 7 cm

YOUNG STARTER
see ingredients on page 113

DOUGH
450 g water
50 g young starter
5 g fresh organic baking yeast
10 g honey
250 g whole-grain barley flour
250 g bread flour
10 g salt

YOUNG STARTER
Refresh your stock starter 8–12 hours before use (see page 113).

DOUGH
Combine all the ingredients and mix the dough as described on pages 108–9.

Pour the dough into the greased loaf tin and leave to rise for at least 12 hours as described on page 110.

Bake the bread following the instructions on page 110, for approximately 40–45 minutes.

DARK WHOLE-GRAIN BREAD WITH MALT AND BERRIES POACHED IN BEER

Malt adds sweetness and a slightly chargrilled taste to this bread, the beer adds a sour note and the berries add fullness and succulence. And not only that, this loaf stays fresh for days. Serve for lunch or use in packed lunches or as a filling snack-bread.

1 loaf of bread, baked in a tin measuring 25 x 12 x 7 cm

YOUNG STARTER
see ingredients on page 113

BERRIES
200 g grain berries (regular or heritage, rye or barley)
300 g dark beer
100 g water
10 g salt

DOUGH
450 g water
50 g young starter
5 g fresh organic baking yeast
10 g honey
20 g malt syrup
250 g whole-grain wheat flour
250 g bread flour
10 g salt

TOPPING
wheat flakes

YOUNG STARTER
Refresh your stock starter 8–12 hours before use (see page 113).

BERRIES
Add the ingredients to a saucepan over a high heat. Bring to the boil, then reduce the heat and simmer until the grain berries are tender. This should take 30–40 minutes, depending on the type of grain berries you use. Drain the cooked grain berries and add them to a container with a lid. Cover and leave to cool in the fridge.

DOUGH
Combine all the ingredients, except the grain berries, and mix the dough as described on pages 108–9. When you've finished mixing the dough, add the grain berries and mix until evenly distributed. This will take 1–2 minutes in a food stand mixer on low speed.

Pour the dough into a greased baking tin and leave to rise for at least 12 hours as described on page 110.

Sprinkle the loaf with wheat flakes and bake following the instructions on page 110, for approximately 40–45 minutes.

SWEET WHOLE-GRAIN BREAD WITH RAISINS SOAKED IN CIDER VINEGAR

Perhaps you're wondering why we add vinegar to this dough. The reason is that the vinegar's perfect sweet-and-sour balance underpins both the sourness of the natural starter and the sweetness of the syrup. Once the raisins have absorbed the vinegar, they impart an explosive flavour, enhanced even further by the addition of caraway seeds.

1 loaf of bread, baked in a tin measuring 25 x 12 x 7 cm

YOUNG STARTER
see ingredients on page 113

RAISINS IN VINEGAR
150 g raisins
25 g cider vinegar
25 g water
15 g roasted caraway seeds

DOUGH
450 g water
50 g young starter
5 g organic fresh baking yeast
100 g golden syrup
250 g whole-grain wheat flour
250 g bread flour
10 g salt

YOUNG STARTER
Refresh your stock starter 8–12 hours before use (see page 113).

RAISINS IN VINEGAR
Place the raisins, vinegar, and water in a saucepan over a high heat and leave to boil until the raisins have absorbed all the liquid. Stir in the caraway seeds and transfer the mixture to a container with a lid. Cover and place in the fridge to cool until you are ready to use it.

DOUGH
Combine all the ingredients, except the raisins, and mix the dough as described on pages 108–9. When you've finished mixing the dough, add the raisins and mix until evenly distributed. This will take 1–2 minutes in a food stand mixer on low speed.

Pour the dough into the greased loaf tin and leave to rise as described on page 110, for at least 12 hours.

Sprinkle the loaf with wheat flakes and bake following the instructions on page 110, for approximately 40–45 minutes.

WHAT'S WRONG WITH MY WHOLE-GRAIN BREAD – AND HOW DO I FIX IT?

Things don't always go according to plan when baking bread, so we've provided you with a guide to some of the most common problems you'll come across when you bake whole-grain bread. This guide will help you solve any problems as they arise so you'll know what to watch out for next time around.

Please note that there may be several reasons for the same problem and sometimes, there might even be directly opposing reasons behind the same issue. When this happens, you may have to consider which reason is most likely to have caused your specific problem or perhaps try to correct several different things at once.

MY BREAD IS STICKY IN THE MIDDLE

Your bread is not done
Measure the bread temperature using the probe of a kitchen thermometer next time you bake. Once the core temperature has reached 98–100°C the bread is done.

Your dough has not risen sufficiently
Leave your dough to rise for at little longer next time you bake.

MY BREAD IS TOO SOUR

You left your dough to rise for too long
Reduce the rising time next time you bake.

You left your young starter for too long after refreshing it, which has turned it sour
Don't leave your young starter at room temperature for too long before you add it to your dough. If you sense that the young starter is too sour before you add it to the dough, you can simply add a little less.

Your bread is not done
Bread that is under-baked may generate excess sourness. Use a kitchen thermometer next time you bake. Once the core temperature has reached 98–100°C the bread is done.

THERE ARE HOLES UNDERNEATH THE CRUST AND A DENSE CRUMB AT THE BOTTOM OF MY BREAD

Your dough has been left to rise for too long (in the fridge)

This will make the crust settle quickly after placing the dough in the oven, as the dough immediately beneath the crust will be too porous and drop to the bottom part of the bread during baking. Next time, leave the dough to rise for a shorter period of time to make it less porous and to leave it with a little power to rise that final bit once it's in the oven.

High oven temperature combined with dough that's too cold

Leave the dough in its container at room temperature for a short while before baking.

Your dough has not risen sufficiently before going into the oven

Insufficient rising time will cause the top to react to the heat-shock and rise quickly. Leave the dough to rise a little longer next time you bake.

If you notice that your dough doesn't rise as much as it should while in the fridge, take the container out of the fridge and set it somewhere warm, for example, on top of a radiator. This will stimulate the yeast cells into action before the loaf has to go into the oven.

MY BREAD CRUMB IS TOO DENSE

Your dough has not risen sufficiently

Make sure your dough rises by 50 per cent. If you notice that your dough doesn't rise as much as it should while in the fridge, you can take the container out of the fridge and leave it somewhere warm, such as on top of a radiator, which will kick the yeast cells into action before the bread has to go into the oven.

Your dough has over-risen

If you've let the dough rise for too long its structure will have become porous and the dough will tend to collapse a little as you chop it into smaller portions and place it in the oven. Next time leave the dough to rise for a shorter period of time.

If you notice that your dough rises more than it should, you can always save it by punching it down before pouring it into another greased loaf tin and letting it rise again. But this time around, it's important that it rises optimally (see page 110).

You haven't mixed your dough enough

Mix it some more (see page 280). Further mixing will strengthen the gluten strands and enable them to hold on to the carbon dioxide generated by the yeast cells, which will leave bigger holes in the crumb. If you're in doubt as to whether or not your dough needs more mixing, perform the gluten test (see page 281), before letting the dough rise.

RYE BREAD

Rye bread is dark and acidulous with a soft crumb and a sweet aroma; for hundreds of years it was a staple food here in Scandinavia. It can be made simply with whole-grain rye flour, natural starter, salt and water. It tastes absolutely fantastic, but there are many ways you can vary both the taste and texture.

RYE BREAD

Rye is really well suited to a climate with cool, damp summers. It was originally regarded only as a weed that grew in wheat fields, but it proved tenacious and difficult to get rid of. In the end, even the Vikings surrendered and turned it into one of our all-time favourite grains, for which we owe them a debt of gratitude!

Studies of Danish eating habits reveal that since the 1970s, the consumption of rye bread has been steadily declining, while consumption of white bread has increased. We would like to change this. Rye bread is high in fibre and thus wonderfully filling and it invigorates the senses. And with its sweet-and-sour aroma it goes so well with cold cuts and all kinds of sandwich spreads.

Personally, I believe that the predominant flavour in rye bread should be rye. You can buy numerous different types of rye bread where rye flour has in fact been substituted with wheat flour, but that only diminishes the lovely taste of genuine rye,

and it also makes the bread less characteristic and less tasty. So, at Meyer's Bakeries we add as much rye to our dough as possible to preserve that pure rye flavour in our bread.

Rye flour doesn't have the same type of gluten as wheat flour, so while it's not difficult to make tasty rye bread, the dough must be worked a little differently than wheat or whole-grain dough. Fortunately, rye flour contains a polysaccharide, called pentosan. This is significant for rye dough in two ways because it binds the carbon dioxide developed by the wild yeast cells and lactic acid bacteria in a natural starter, which then enables the dough to rise,

and it also binds liquids, which help make the rye bread soft and tender.

In other words, rye flour is without a shadow of a doubt the most important ingredient in the following recipes, not least the basic rye bread recipe, which contains only rye-starter, whole-grain rye flour, salt and water. In addition, you also get recipes with lots of variations in taste and texture. If you like you can add malt or honey, as well as different seeds and berries, or you can try the wonderfully tasty *svedjerug* or slash-and-burn rye bread on page 159.

STARTER

When you bake rye bread you need an active and potent rye starter to help your rye bread rise while imparting it with a delicate acidity. On page 39, we tell you how to get hold of some natural starter or how to make your own. You can also find out how you change wheat starter into rye starter, and how you make it as potent as possible.

REFRESH YOUR STARTER

The day before you want to actually bake your rye bread, you need to refresh your rye stock starter to make sure it's completely up and running and able to help your rye dough rise.

Take your rye stock starter from the fridge and refresh with rye flour and water (see page 41) to turn it into young starter. Leave at room temperature. Once its surface starts bubbling and frothing, after 12–24 hours, the starter is 'awake' and ready to be put to use. Take out the amount you want to use for baking, and put the rest back in the fridge (or keep it at room temperature, depending on when you next expect to bake rye bread). This will be your new rye stock starter (read more about this on pages 37–49). If you're not convinced that your rye starter is up to the job, you can always add 1 tablespoon of fresh baking yeast to the final dough.

INGREDIENTS

In addition to the starter we only use rye flour, salt and water in our basic rye bread recipe. The gluten in rye flour is different from that in wheat flour, and it doesn't bind as well, which is something you should remember when mixing your rye dough.

FLOUR

The rye flour we use in our recipes is 100 per cent rye flour, with every bit of bran and germ included. So even if rye flour doesn't contain gluten strands, its high content of pentosan (see page 140), ensures that it can still rise. And you end up with tender rather than damp, soggy bread.

WATER

As we have explained, rye flour is a type of whole-grain flour with the bran and germ included. This means it can absorb huge amounts of water, compared to regular sifted flour. This high level of hydration yields a very 'wet' dough and wonderfully succulent bread.

SALT

Salt slows down the propagation of wild yeast cells in your natural starter, which prolongs the rising time and stimulates the flour's baking ability. This is all to the advantage as the flavours are allowed time to fully develop, the crumb opens, and the texture of the bread is improved.

We use fine salt, which dissolves easily, but you can also use fine sea salt or Himalayan salt from a salt grinder, if you want extra minerals and flavour.

MIX YOUR DOUGH AND POUR IT INTO A LOAF TIN

As mentioned, rye flour doesn't contain gluten strands, so when you make rye dough, the aim is to mix all the ingredients and make the dough as homogeneous as possible. And as you also want your rye dough to be as hydrated as possible to ensure a tender crumb, baking rye bread in a loaf tin is usually the best option.

#TIP

You can put a piece of nonstick baking paper in the loaf tin if you want to make sure you'll be able to get the finished loaf out in one piece rather than in bits and pieces, which are then impossible to slice. Grease the loaf tin with a little butter and then line the tin with nonstick baking paper. The butter will help the paper adhere to the inside of the tin. Once the rye bread is done, the loaf can be removed from the tin by lifting out the paper.

HOW TO MIX RYE DOUGH

1. Put the young rye starter and water into a bowl and stir.

2. Add the flour and salt.

3. Using a wooden spoon, mix the ingredients for 4–5 minutes, or until you have a homogenous, wet dough. If you are using a food stand mixer it will require less mixing time.

4. Grease the loaf tin well with butter, reaching into all the corners and leaving no bare spots (this will make it easier to remove the finished loaf from the tin). Fill the baking tin two-thirds full of dough, leaving enough room for it to rise. Smooth the top with a wet rubber spatula or your wet palm.

5. Cover the tin with a plastic food bag cut open and attached with an elastic band. Leave the rye bread to rise until it has increased by 30–50 per cent.

#TIP
Keep an eye on the dough as it rises. It's ready to be baked when there are six or seven pin-sized holes in the surface.

PROVING YOUR RYE DOUGH

When baking rye bread it's important to use your eyes and not just rely on your watch to decide when the rising time is over. As mentioned, rye dough must increase in size by 30–50 per cent in the tin before baking and this can take anything from 2–6 hours. The timing will depend on how active your natural starter is, how warm the room is, and the texture of the dough. Once the surface begins to crack and five or six tiny pin-sized holes appear, immediately slide the loaf tin into the oven.

The key to success is to leave the dough to rise for the right amount of time – neither too long nor too short – before sliding it into the hot oven. If your bread hasn't risen sufficiently before going into the oven it will crack, and if it's been left for too long it can collapse once it's in the oven, and there will be a hollow just underneath the crust. Resist the temptation to let your rye dough rise just that little bit longer in the hope that your finished bread will be that bit bigger and more beautiful.

BAKING YOUR RYE BREAD

Preheat your oven to its maximum temperature, giving it plenty of time to reach the required heat. You can use your oven's fan-assisted function, if available, to speed up the heating process.

Place the rye bread in the hot oven and leave the fan function on for the initial 10 minutes. Then reduce the heat to 180°C, Gas Mark 4, and bake until finished.

Giving exact baking times for rye bread can be a bit of challenge but expect it to take 50–60 minutes. Ovens vary greatly in terms of heat distribution and you can't necessarily trust the thermostat. Rye bread sizes and shapes also vary, which is why a digital kitchen thermometer is so useful for checking if your bread is done. After the loaf has been baking for 40–45 minutes insert the thermometer's probe into the centre of the bread. When the temperature reaches 97°C, the bread is done. Leaving the bread in the oven too long will make the crumb dry.

LEAVE YOUR RYE BREAD TO COOL

There are two different ways to let your rye bread cool, depending on whether you want a crisp or a soft crust. If you want a crisp crust, carefully tip the bread out of the tin and onto a rack to cool. For a soft crust, take the bread out of the tin and set it aside but after about 10 minutes return it to the tin it was baked in. The bread will generate steam, which turns into moisture that softens the crust. It's easier to slice rye bread with a soft crust, and children seem to prefer this version as well.

If you can, wait until the following day before you slice the bread. If not, leave it for at least 6–8 hours, even if it is difficult to resist the temptation to dive right in. Freshly baked rye bread needs time to settle before it can be nicely sliced, and you won't be able to assess whether your crumb is too damp, too dry, or just perfect until some time has passed.

STORING RYE BREAD

Rye bread stays moist and soft at room temperature or a little below. It does not like being kept in the fridge, because at 5°C the crumb begins to crystallize (read more about this on page 286), and this will make the bread seem dry when eating it. But on the other hand, your bread will last longer if it's kept in the fridge. So, if you bake two loaves, you could keep one at room temperature and store the other in the fridge until the first one is finished. And it's worth keeping in mind that toasting a slice of rye bread will neutralize the crystallization.

#TIP

Use a digital kitchen thermometer the first couple of times you bake rye bread until you get a feel for how your oven works and how much time is needed.

CLASSIC RYE BREAD

Here's a recipe for a basic, straightforward loaf of rye bread, made only with rye flour, natural starter, water and salt, with no added ingredients such as seeds or berries. With no other ingredients to overpower the delicate taste of the rye, you'll get a lovely, moist bread with a distinct rye flavour. So, if you're one of those people who usually prefers white bread, now's your chance to try out a wonderful, home-baked rye bread. It'll stay fresh for days, that is, if you haven't eaten it all by then!

2 loaves, each baked in a tin measuring
25 x 12 x 7 cm

YOUNG STARTER
150 g rye stock starter
300 g lukewarm water
195 g rye flour

DOUGH
400 g young starter
800 g lukewarm water
850 g rye flour
20 g salt

YOUNG STARTER
Refresh your rye stock starter 12–24 hours before use (see page 141). Mix the ingredients in a small bowl and leave at room temperature, covered with a lid or a tea towel, until the surface starts to froth and tastes a little sour. The longer you leave the starter the more sour it will become (as will your rye bread). Taste the starter every so often to find how just how sour you want your rye bread to be.

The portion of young starter you don't use will now become your new rye stock starter, so save it for the next time you want to bake bread (see diagram on page 39).

DOUGH
Mix together all the ingredients. See pages 142–4 for how to mix your dough before pouring it into the greased loaf tins and leaving it to rise. Rising times may vary between 2–6 hours – see instructions on pages 144–5.

Bake the bread following the instructions on page 145, for approximately 50–60 minutes.

#TIP
Though highly unlikely, if you should find yourself incapable of eating all your rye bread, you can make really delicious rye bread croutons, which are lovely in salads or sprinkled on soups. You can also use sweet sugar-roasted rye bread croutons in layered cakes or with ice cream, on top of sour dairy products or as part of a filling in an old-fashioned apple or rhubarb Charlotte.

DARK MALT RYE BREAD

In this recipe we add malt to our basic dough. Malt is made from sprouted barley that's been chargrilled and is available either as flour or syrup. It imparts a delicious, slightly chargrilled flavour and a darker colour to the rye bread.

2 loaves, each baked in a tin measuring
25 x 12 x 7 cm

YOUNG STARTER
see ingredients on page 147

DOUGH
400 g young starter
800 g lukewarm water
10 g dark malt flour or 30 g malt syrup
850 g rye flour
20 g salt

YOUNG STARTER
Refresh your rye stock starter 12–24 hours before use (see page 141).

DOUGH
Mix together all the ingredients. See pages 142–4 for how to mix your dough before pouring it into the greased loaf tins and letting it rise. Rising time may vary between 2 to 6 hours – see instructions on pages 144–5.

Bake the bread following the instructions on page 145, for approximately 50–60 minutes.

MEYER'S DARK RYE BREAD WITH RYE BERRIES AND PUMPKIN SEEDS

This is one of my personal favourites, and it's also the most popular rye bread in our bakeries. It's a light and tender loaf that stays fresh for a long time. Here, the fabulous, intense taste of dark malt and rye is supplemented by the lovely crunchiness of pumpkin seeds. If you can't get your hands on cut rye berries, which give the bread a chewy bite, you can just as easily use cracked rye berries.

2 loaves, each baked in a tin measuring 25 x 12 x 7 cm

YOUNG STARTER
see ingredients on page 147

BERRIES AND SEEDS
340 g cracked rye berries
175 g pumpkin seeds
500 g cold water

DOUGH
400 g young starter
200 g lukewarm water
10 g dark malt flour or 30 g malt syrup
400 g rye flour
20 g salt

YOUNG STARTER
Refresh your rye stock starter 12–24 hours before use (see page 141).

BERRIES AND SEEDS
At the same time that you refresh your natural stock starter, 12–24 hours before baking, mix the cut rye berries and pumpkin seeds in a bowl and add the water. Cover and leave at room temperature.

DOUGH
Mix together all the dough ingredients. Drain the soaked berries and seeds and mix them into the dough.

See pages 142–4 for how to mix your dough before pouring it into the greased loaf tins and leaving it to rise. Rising time may vary between 2–6 hours – see instructions on pages 144–5.

Bake the bread following the instructions on page 145, for approximately 50–60 minutes.

SPICED RYE BREAD WITH BARLEY BERRIES

A visit to the mill Saltå Kvarn, in Järna, just outside Stockholm was the inspiration for this recipe. At Saltå Kvarn they only mill local, organically grown grain and use stone mills. In medieval times, it was quite common to bake bread with barley flour. These days, you rarely come across a loaf of bread that contains much barley, and this is probably due to the difficulties of baking only with barley, as explained on page 31. In this recipe, however, we use tender, boiled barley berries, which are easy to work with yet still have that lovely barley flavour. We add a little extra character to the bread by adding aniseed or fennel seeds, which gives a piquant snack-bread that goes really well with all kinds of sandwich spreads.

2 loaves, each baked in a tin measuring
25 x 12 x 7 cm

YOUNG STARTER
see ingredients on page 147

BERRIES
200 g barley berries

DOUGH
400 g young starter
500 g lukewarm water
100 g honey
570 g rye flour
200 g bread flour
20 g salt
10 g crushed fennel seeds
  or crushed aniseeds

YOUNG STARTER
Refresh your rye stock starter 12–24 hours before use (see page 141).

BERRIES
Twelve hours before you intend to make the rye dough, boil the berries in plenty of lightly salted water for about 20 minutes, or until they are tender. Drain the berries, rinse in cold water, and leave to chill in the fridge before use.

DOUGH
Combine all the dough ingredients and then stir in the prepared barley berries.

See pages 142–4 for how to mix your dough before pouring it into the greased loaf tins and leaving it to rise. Rising time may vary between 2–6 hours—see instructions on pages 144–5.

Bake the bread following the instructions on page 145, for approximately 50–60 minutes.

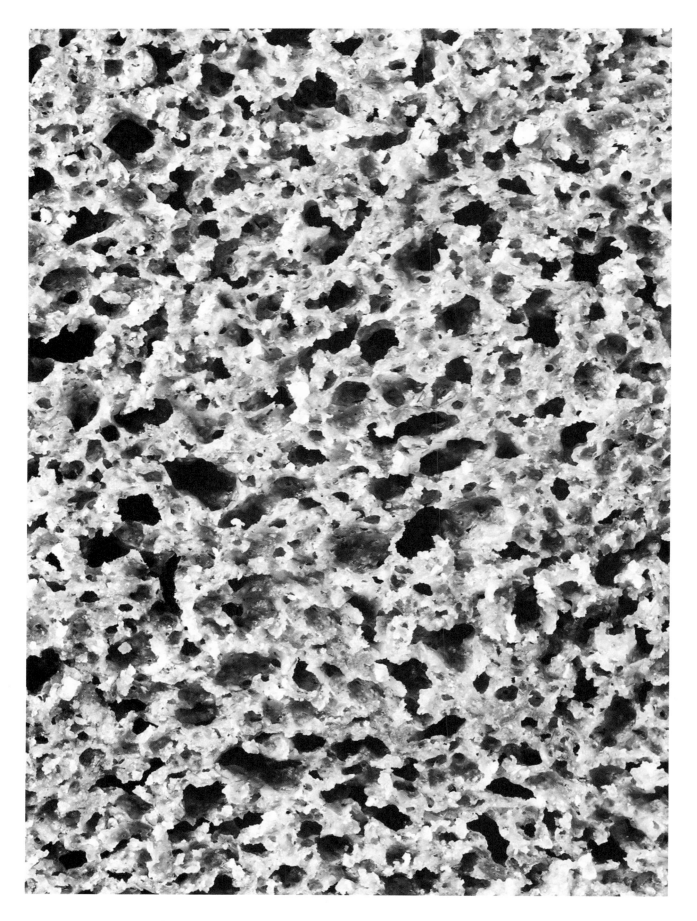

SLASH-AND-BURN RYE BREAD (SVEDJERUG)

Slash-and-burn rye bread (also known as *svedjerug*) uses a Nordic heritage rye, which is enjoying something of a renaissance here in Scandinavia (read more on page 30). You use the flour in much the same way you would regular rye flour, but it's a little finer and more complex in flavour, and its protein content is twice that of regular rye flour. The result is a tender loaf of bread that will keep fresher for longer. If you cannot find slash-and-burn rye, regular rye flour will work just as well.

2 loaves, each baked in a tin measuring
25 x 12 x 7 cm

SLASH-AND-BURN STARTER
150 g rye stock starter
300 g lukewarm water
195 g slash-and-burn rye flour

DOUGH
400 g young slash-and-burn rye starter
800 g lukewarm water
850 g slash-and-burn rye flour
20 g salt

YOUNG STARTER
Refresh your rye stock starter with slash-and-burn rye flour 12–24 hours before use (see page 141).

DOUGH
Combine all the ingredients. See pages 142–4 for how to mix your dough before pouring it into the greased loaf tins and leaving it to rise. Rising time may vary between 2–6 hours—see instructions on pages 144–5.

Bake the bread following the instructions on page 145, for approximately 50–60 minutes.

SWEDISH SYRUP LOAF WITH ALMONDS AND PRUNES

The first time I tasted this bread was at a small family-run beachfront hotel in Arild, in Sweden. The chef told me which ingredients he used, but he didn't specify the measurements, which is why I don't use specific measures when I bake these loaves. However, for this recipe, I measured out what I actually put into the dough and have given the quantities here. This bread is absolutely fantastic (it also makes great toast), spread with a little butter or a lovely, salty blue cheese, or anything else you'd usually enjoy with rye bread. Kids love the delicate sweetness of this bread.

2 loaves, each baked in a tin measuring
25 x 12 x 7 cm

YOUNG STARTER
see ingredients on page 147

DOUGH
400 g young starter
600 g lukewarm water
250 g molasses
700 g rye flour
200 g bread flour
20 g salt
200 g roughly chopped prunes
150 g roughly chopped blanched almonds

YOUNG STARTER
Refresh your rye stock starter 12–24 hours before use (see page 141).

DOUGH
Combine all the ingredients. See pages 142–4 for how to mix your dough before pouring it into the loaf tins and leaving it to rise. Rising time may vary between 2–6 hours—see instructions on pages 144–5.

Bake the bread following the instructions on page 145, for approximately 50–60 minutes.

#TIP
You can use your favourite basic dough recipe and simply add prunes, almonds and syrup and then keep adding rye flour until you have the right texture.

FILLED RYE BARS

This is the recipe for one of the best-selling snacks in Meyer's Bakeries. You can vary the bars according to taste, depending on what's in season. You will need ten mini loaf tins measuring 10 x 3.5 x 2.5 cm, but you could also bake them in a muffin tin.

Makes 10 bars, each baked in a mini loaf tin measuring 10 x 3.5 x 2.5 cm

DOUGH
1 kg of any type of rye dough, such as Meyer's Dark Rye Bread with Rye Berries and Pumpkin Seeds (see page 153). Please note that the recipe makes 2 kg of dough, so use half the quantities given on page 153 to yield enough dough for the Filled Rye Bars.

SUGGESTED FILLINGS
50 g dates
100 g whole hazelnuts

OR
150 g hard cheese, such as Manchego

OR
50 g dried cranberries
100 g walnuts

OR
150 g plain chocolate, preferably 85 per cent cocoa solids

Chop or slice the filling ingredients you have chosen into smaller pieces and set them aside. Knead the rye dough and then mix in the chopped ingredients.

Pour the dough into the (greased) tins and leave to rise for 30 minutes.

Bake the bars in an oven preheated to 180°C, Gas Mark 4, for 30 minutes. Leave them to cool for a while in the mini loaf tins before transferring to a rack to finish cooling.

#TIP
Place a roasting tin in the bottom of the oven while it preheats. When you place the bars in the oven, pour 100 g of water into the hot roasting tin. The steam created will give the finished bars a beautiful sheen.

LEFTOVER RYE BREAD

Why throw away dried-out bits of rye bread when you can bring them back to life in a freshly baked rye bread? Just soak them overnight and the next day they are ready for use. It's so simple.

INGREDIENTS
200 g leftover rye bread, broken into pieces
300 g light beer or water

Place the rye bread pieces in a bowl. Add the light beer or water to cover the bread and leave for a few hours or overnight to soak.

Pour the mixture into a sieve and leave to drain for a few minutes. Then squeeze the rye bread with your fingers to get rid of as much liquid as possible.

The soaked rye bread is now ready to be added to any one of the other rye bread recipes.

#TIP
If you have more than the quantity of leftover rye bread called for here, keep adding enough water or light beer to cover.

WHAT'S WRONG WITH MY RYE BREAD – AND HOW DO I FIX IT?

Things don't always go according to plan when baking rye bread, and below you'll find a guide to some of the most common problems you might encounter. Use this guide to try and solve the problems as they arise so you'll know what to watch out for next time around.

Remember that there may be several reasons for the same problem and sometimes, there might even be directly opposing reasons behind it. When this happens, you'll need to consider what factor is most likely to have caused your specific problem or try to correct several things all at once.

MY BREAD IS SOGGY WHEN I SLICE IT
You tried to slice it too soon. Remember that you won't get a proper sense of the texture of a freshly baked loaf of rye bread until it's been allowed to rest until it is completely cool.

Your bread is still too hot
Leave your bread to rest for at least 12 hours before slicing it the next time you bake.

Your bread is not done
Check the temperature of the centre of the bread using the probe of a kitchen thermometer next time you bake to ensure it has reached 97°C, at which point the bread will be done.

If you don't have a thermometer, leave the bread in the oven a little longer next time. With rye bread, it's better to give it 10 minutes more than taking it out too early. This may result in a slightly harder crust, but you'll avoid the soggy crumb.

Your rye flour may have been sprout-damaged, resulting in a dough that's not acidulous enough
Try adding a little more natural starter next time you bake, substitute some of the rye flour with whole-grain flour and make sure you add enough salt to your dough. (Read more on page 278.)

The dough's too wet, and can't absorb all the liquid
Try adding a little more flour next time. If you find the dough a little thinner than usual as you're mixing it, add a little extra rye flour. This might eliminate a very wet and sticky crumb.

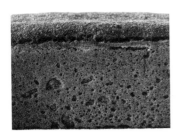

THE SIDES OF THE LOAF CRACK WHILE BAKING

Your dough has not risen sufficiently before going into the oven

The crust dries out in the oven, and as there is still plenty of rising power in the bread, it will crack the dried surface and this prevents the bread from rising optimally. Let the dough increase a little in size next time, before sliding it into the oven to bake.

If you're not sure whether or not your dough has risen sufficiently, you can always look for the pin-sized holes that appear on the surface. There should be six or seven of them by the time you slide the dough into the oven (see page 144).

The oven was too dry

Place a roasting tin in the bottom of the oven while it is preheating. Pour 100 g of water into the tin immediately after sliding in the bread to generate a bit of steam and moisture inside the oven.

THERE ARE HOLES UNDERNEATH THE CRUST AND A SOGGY CRUMB UNDERNEATH

Your dough has been left to rise for too long before going into the oven

When dough rises for too long, its texture becomes porous and loose, and it collapses easily. Don't leave your dough to rise for as long next time. While your dough should rise nicely in the loaf tins, it should still retain a little power for rising in the oven. (See when to place your bread in the oven on page 145.)

If you notice that your dough rises more than it should, you can always rescue it by punching it down before pouring it into another greased loaf tin and leaving it to rise again. But this time around, it's important that it rises optimally, and not for too long or too briefly (see page 145).

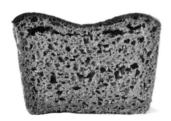

MY BREAD COLLAPSES INTO A U-SHAPE ON TOP

Your dough's over-hydrated

Add a little more flour next time you bake to make the dough firmer. If you sense that the dough is too wet as you go along, simply add a little more rye flour.

Your bread is not done

Insert the probe of a kitchen thermometer into the centre of the loaf to check the core temperature. When it has reached 97°C, the bread is done. If you don't have a thermometer, simply bake the bread a little longer next time.

MY BREAD IS TOO SOUR

You left your young starter for too long after refreshing it, which has turned it sour

Don't leave your young starter at room temperature for too long before adding it to your dough.

Your bread is not done

If your bread isn't completely done when you take it out of the oven, it may generate excess acidity. Use the probe of a kitchen thermometer next time you bake to check that the core temperature has reached 97°C before you take the bread out of the oven.

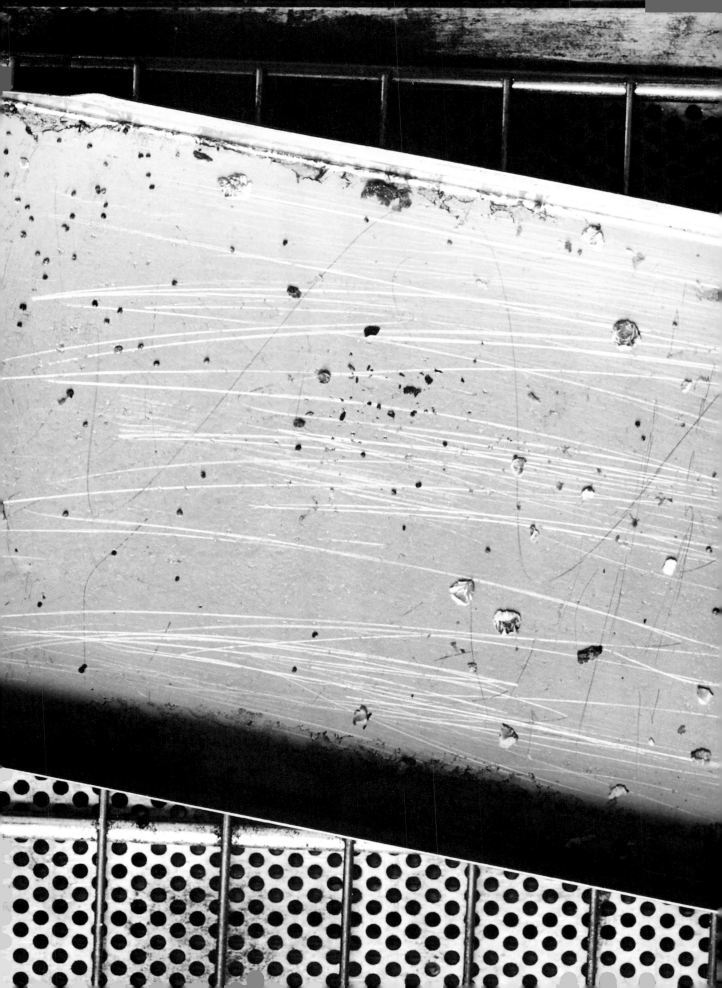

ENRICHED DOUGH

Soft buns, brown sugar bread as well as sinful, succulent pastries such as sticky buns and Christmas cakes can all be made using enriched dough. Burger buns and scones made with homemade enriched dough far outdo the ready-baked kind – so make plenty!

ENRICHED DOUGH

Long-rise bread with whole-grain flour is lovely, hearty and highly nutritious, but occasionally, we feel like eating something else. Sometimes, we get an insatiable craving for sweet-smelling cinnamon buns, succulent soft buns or a slice of cinnamon loaf with marzipan and cinnamon filling that simply melts on your tongue.

This is where plain flour takes the lead. We use it in buns, rolls, cakes and sweet pastries, in other words, everything light and audacious. And anyway, you only ever eat chocolate pastry for the sheer pleasure of it, never to improve your physical health!

You can use stone-milled presifted flour, which will invariably contain tiny bits of bran and germ. However, this will give you a slightly denser crumb and a slightly healthier pastry. And most important of all, you get a more pronounced flavour of the grain.

Working with enriched dough (also referred to as soft dough) is highly pleasurable. The final ingredient you knead into the dough is butter, and once the dough has rested, you roll it out, fold it and shape according to what you're baking. Shaping Cinnamon Swirls may take a little practice, but don't worry. Participants at our baking courses regularly go home with a bag full of perfectly shaped Cinnamon Swirls at the end of the day, despite their earlier attempts. Follow the recipe and the step-by-step photos on pages 199–203. Practice will make perfect, and we are pretty certain your family won't mind eating misshapen pastries until you're able to produce beautifully shaped, shiny and aromatic Cinnamon Swirls.

Opposite, we present you with the basic principles of how to make enriched dough. We'll take you through the ingredients, followed by the kneading, resting, shaping, rising and baking processes. We'll provide you with a basic recipe with a little less butter for soft buns and brown sugar bread, for example, and another basic dough with lots of butter that can be turned into succulent, sinful sticky buns and Christmas cakes. In addition, this chapter also contains recipes for sausage rolls, burger buns and scones that are so much better than what is available to buy in supermarkets – so make plenty!

HOW TO MAKE ENRICHED DOUGH

1. Measure the ingredients and leave until they reach room temperature

2. Mix the ingredients and knead the dough until shiny and smooth

3. Add butter and finish kneading

4. Leave the dough to rest

5. Shape the dough and leave to rise

6. Bake the dough

INGREDIENTS

If you're not used to baking, always start by measuring the different ingredients separately and then line them up, one after the other. This will help ensure you don't omit anything.

THE INGREDIENTS SHOULD BE AT ROOM TEMPERATURE

When you make enriched dough, it's better if the ingredients have reached room temperature before you start mixing them to enable the dough to rise more quickly. A huge lump of cold dough has to warm up before it can actually begin to rise.

It is particularly important that the butter is at room temperature. Dough absorbs soft butter much more quickly, and you risk over-mixing if you use cold butter.

FLOUR

In enriched dough, we primarily use milled wheat flour with hardly any bran or germ. This flour consists almost exclusively of endosperm, which contains starch and protein. This produces strong gluten strands, which enable the dough to rise beautifully (read more about wheat flour and gluten on pages 280–1).

YEAST

We use more baking yeast in our enriched dough than in any of our other kinds of dough and as we only use regular plain flour, it doesn't need to rise for very long. However, longer rising times impart Wheat Buns, Ambrosia Cube Cakes and Nordic Kringles with the sweetness that makes children ask for more and adults ask for the recipe. In addition, longer rising times allow you to prepare your dough a day in advance.

At Meyer's Bakeries, we always use fresh organic baking yeast because it contains different yeast strains than conventional yeast. This is also why it tastes a little different (read more about yeast on page 282).

SUGAR

In our enriched dough recipes, unless otherwise stated we use organic cane sugar. It doesn't dissolve as easily as white sugar, but you can't beat the taste. If you use high-quality caster sugar, however, you'll also get good results. In addition to sweetness, sugar also acts as a nutrient for yeast cells and so influences the rising times. The right quantity of sugar will also enhance the taste of the other ingredients and add colour to your finished pastries.

BUTTER

First and foremost, butter imparts your pastries with an absolutely fantastic taste as well as enhancing its beautifully golden colour. Butter is also the reason that pastries are so tender and soft, as opposed to wheat bread, for example, which we prefer to be more chewy. While unsalted is often used in baking, we always use salted butter as we think it tastes better and you don't have to add salt to the recipe.

We do not add butter to our dough until after kneading, when it's already in the process of producing the gluten strands that will bind the dough and contain the fluids until we bake it. Once butter is added and as it warms up from further kneading, it will envelop the gluten strands and 'grease' them, which makes them even more expandable, and this will make your finished dough rise even more beautifully.

EGGS

We add eggs to our dough for extra softness as well as taste. Eggs act as a leavening agent, give the dough even shinier surfaces, and help keep the finished pastries fresher longer.

MILK

There are two reasons for adding milk to enriched dough: it imparts the finished pastry with a rounded taste and it gives it a darker colour. We recommend that you use organic whole milk because it actually tastes like real milk. In terms of texture and crumb, you should always use milk with a high percentage of fat. However, we do not recommend substituting cream for milk.

HOW TO KNEAD ENRICHED DOUGH IN A STAND MIXER

1. Add water (or milk) and yeast to the bowl of a food stand mixer and stir until the yeast dissolves. Crack the eggs into the bowl and mix them in.

2. Add the flour and sugar and knead well on low speed until the dough is smooth, shiny and effortlessly comes away from the inside of the bowl, a sure sign that the dough has developed gluten strands. This should take 6–8 minutes, depending on your machine's power.

3. Chop the butter into small cubes and add it all at once.

4. Knead the dough well, until all the butter is absorbed and the dough is once again shiny and smooth. When it slides off the inside of the bowl stop the machine immediately. Once the butter settles around the gluten strands, making them more expandable, they also become more vulnerable and they will break if you continue kneading the dough.

HOW TO KNEAD ENRICHED DOUGH BY HAND

1. If you're not afraid to work up a sweat, knead your enriched dough by hand. Start off by combining the ingredients together in a bowl, including the butter.

2. Knead the dough thoroughly. The butter is absorbed somewhat more slowly when you knead by hand. Once you've given the dough a good knead in the bowl, tip it out onto your work surface and knead it well for another 6–8 minutes.

3. Return the dough to the bowl and leave to rest for 5 minutes, after which knead it for another 2 minutes.

LET THE DOUGH REST

It's important that you leave the dough to rest, both when kneading it in a food stand mixer or by hand. You can leave it somewhere cool, such as in the fridge, or somewhere warm, such as on the kitchen table (if you want to use it straightaway). Resting time lets the dough absorb the last drops of fluid and 'take time out' as its gluten strands have been pulled and stretched during kneading, and they need a rest. You'll witness a slight contraction in the dough – a bit like pulling on an elastic band – if you start shaping it straightaway and don't leave it time to rest.

Seal the dough in clingfilm or put it in a plastic container and cover it with a lid or clingfilm. Leave in the fridge or on the kitchen table.

It should be left for no more than 30 minutes to 1 hour on the kitchen table but remain overnight in the fridge. Depending on what you're actually baking, placing the dough somewhere cool could turn into an advantage as cold dough is easier to handle than lukewarm dough. Be aware that after shaping, cold dough needs a longer rising time than warm dough.

SHAPING AND RISING YOUR ENRICHED DOUGH

Once your dough is rested, it's time to make Cinnamon Swirls or Soft Buns. Decide on what you want to make beforehand and have any additional creams or fillings ready. You should only have the minimum amount of work to do once the dough is rested. If the dough contracts, it may be stressed because you haven't let it rest for long enough. If that's

the case, simply cover it up and leave to rest for another 5 minutes before continuing. Shape your dough and place it on a greased baking sheet (or one that's lined with nonstick baking paper) and let it rise.

As the dough rises, it also relaxes, which allows the yeast to work. While rising, you should keep an eye on the size of the pastries because they should increase by almost 100 per cent. Rising times will vary depending on the temperature of the dough and the room.

It's important to keep the dough covered while rising to stop its surface drying out and then cracking. If you can't avoid a dry surface all together, you can always brush your pastry with some beaten egg.

#MAKE SPACE

When you bake pastries of any kind, it's important that you make sure that there's plenty of space between them or they'll expand into one another. Leaving some space between the pastries also allows the heat inside the oven to circulate more easily all the way round, so the pastries will bake more evenly.

#USE CLINGFILM

Rather than draping the rising dough with a tea towel, use a piece of clingfilm that has been rubbed on both sides with flour (the flour will keep the clingfilm from crumpling up). Clingfilm weighs nothing and so allows the dough to rise without any resistance. You can save the floured clingfilm in a plastic food bag and reuse it the next time you bake pastries.

BAKING YOUR ENRICHED DOUGH

The oven must be really hot when baking pastries. If your oven has a fan-assisted function, turn it on to help the oven heat more quickly. If you only use one baking sheet at a time, we recommend that you use regular top and bottom heat while baking. If you have more than one baking sheet in the oven at the same time, use the fan-assisted function to keep the heat circulating more evenly.

Most pastries should be brushed with beaten egg before baking, to give them a beautiful sheen.

Be aware that the temperatures and baking times noted in the recipes are only approximate, so always keep an eye on whatever it is you're baking, especially taking note of the colour. If the pastry is turning really dark or seems dry, reduce the heat a little. If necessary, ignore the recommended baking time and remove the pastries from the oven as soon as they seem, feel and smell ready.

STORING AND FREEZING ENRICHED DOUGH AND PASTRIES

If you're planning on baking lots pastries, you can make and shape the dough ahead of time and leave it in the fridge overnight. Then, take the dough out of the fridge for 1–1½ hours to finish rising at room temperature before baking.

You can also freeze pastry dough after shaping it, though how long it keeps will depend on how cold your freezer is and how well the dough is wrapped. Arrange the shaped dough spaced well apart on a baking sheet and leave it for 1–2 hours in the freezer.

Once frozen, transfer the pastries to a sturdy resealable freezer bag and put them back in the freezer. Ensuring that the bags are well sealed will stop the pastry dough absorbing the flavour of any other foods in your freezer.

To thaw, remove the number of pastries you want to bake from the bag in the freezer the day before, spread them out on a baking sheet, then transfer them to the fridge. The following day remove them from the fridge and leave them to rise at room temperature for at least 1½ hours, but preferably longer because freezing the dough may have diminished its rising power.

ENRICHED DOUGH

Below we provide you with a basic enriched dough recipe. Using this, you can make an almost infinite number of recipes, for example Soft Buns, Currant Buns or Brown Sugar Bread. In other words, this dough can be used for anything that calls for a lovely, buttery dough that's not too full of fat.

1 portion

DOUGH
300 g cold water
35 g fresh organic baking yeast
1 egg
625 g plain flour
65 g sugar
10 g salt
50 g salted butter

See pages 173–4 for instructions on how to combine the ingredients and knead the dough.

Cover the bowl with clingfilm and leave to rest at room temperature for 30 minutes, or leave it in the fridge for 2 hours or overnight. Now the dough is ready to shape into whatever type of pastry you wish to bake.

SOFT BUNS

These lovely light buns with a beautiful shiny surface are perfect for birthday parties, with afternoon tea, a cup of coffee or enjoyed on a cold autumn day with a mug of hot chocolate.

10 big buns

DOUGH
see ingredients on page 177

BRUSHING
1 egg

See pages 173–4 for instructions on how to combine the ingredients and knead the dough.

Divide the dough into 10 lumps and shape them into buns. Place the buns on two baking sheets lined with nonstick baking paper. Leave plenty of space between each bun to allow room for them to spread as they rise.

Let the buns rise for 2–3 hours as described on page 174.

Brush the buns with some beaten egg to give them a lovely sheen.

Bake the buns at 200°C, Gas Mark 6, following the instructions on page 175, for approximately 10–12 minutes. Transfer the buns to a rack to cool.

#TIP
Adding some sort of filling to these buns will only make them even better. Try adding 125 g chopped plain chocolate or 125 g sultanas. However, don't add the filling until you've finished kneading the dough.

BROWN SUGAR BREAD

Brown sugar bread, which simply melts on your tongue, is a speciality from the Danish island of Funen. In this recipe we add a little marzipan and cinnamon to the creamed topping and we use the wonderfully aromatic and potent muscovado sugar (a type of very dark brown sugar) for added fullness and flavour. Brown Sugar Bread is best enjoyed while it is still warm.

1 loaf (about 12 servings)

DOUGH
See ingredients page 177

CREAMED TOPPING
100 g sugar
75 g muscovado or very dark
  brown sugar
175 g salted butter, softened
80 g marzipan
25 g golden syrup
25 g molasses
10 g ground cinnamon

CREAMED TOPPING
Add all the ingredients to a bowl and stir to combine. Transfer to a container with a lid, cover and leave at room temperature until ready to use.

DOUGH
See pages 173—4 for instructions on how to mix the ingredients and knead the dough before letting it rest.

Once the dough has rested, roll it out into a 30-cm square. Place the square in a greased baking tin of the same dimensions and use your fingers to make depressions in the dough. Distribute the topping evenly on the surface.

Let the brown sugar bread rise for 2–3 hours as described on page 175.

Bake the brown sugar bread at 200°C, Gas Mark 6, following the instructions on page 175, for approximately 12 minutes.

#TIP
You can also place the baking tin with the dough in the fridge for half an hour before spreading it with the creamed topping. You may find the topping spreads more easily across dough that's not too soft.

LUXURY ENRICHED DOUGH

This dough is very similar to the basic dough on page 177, but we've added more butter and we use whole milk instead of water. This provides us with dough with a higher fat content and a denser texture but with a wonderful buttery taste. This dough is also easier to shape, so you can use it to make cinnamon sticks and loaves as well as many other pastries.

1 portion

DOUGH
200 g cold whole milk
35 g fresh organic baking yeast
1 egg
500 g plain flour
35 g sugar
8 g salt
75 g salted butter

See pages 173–4 for instructions on how to mix the ingredients together and knead the dough. Leave to rest in the fridge for 1 hour.

Once the dough is rested, it's ready for use and can be shaped in any way you like.

CINNAMON LOAF

In my youth, every bakery sold Cinnamon Loaves. The lovely soft dough is stuffed with a butter and cinnamon filling, which results in a different type of sweet bread that can be enjoyed on its own or with an extra sinful layer of butter.

3 small loaves, each baked in an aluminium foil loaf tin measuring 18 x 7 cm

DOUGH
see ingredients on page 182

BUTTER AND CINNAMON FILLING
200 g salted butter
200 g sugar
20 g ground cinnamon

FOR THE BAKING TIN
salted butter
sugar

BRUSHING
1 egg, beaten

FILLING
Add all the ingredients to a bowl and stir to mix. Transfer to a container with a lid, cover and leave at room temperature until ready to use.

DOUGH
See pages 173–4 for instructions on how to mix the ingredients and knead the dough before leaving it to rest.

Once the dough has rested, divide it into three equal lumps and shape them into three loaves as follows: roll one lump of dough into a 30 x 15-cm rectangle. Turn the rectangle so that its short end faces you. Spread one-third of the filling evenly across the dough. Take hold of the short end farthest from you and roll the dough towards you like a Swiss roll.

Generously butter the three aluminium loaf tins and sprinkle the insides with sugar. Place one rolled loaf into each tin. Use a sharp pair of scissors to cut eight 1.5-cm snips into the dough at an angle of 45 degrees. Turn each snip to alternate sides (see photo).

Leave the loaves to rise for 1–2 hours as described on page 174.

Brush the loaves with some beaten egg, then bake at 180°C, Gas Mark 4, following the instructions on page 175 for approximately 20–22 minutes. Transfer to a rack to cool.

CINNAMON STICKS

These Cinnamon Sticks have an added dose of deliciousness because, in addition to the filling used in the Cinnamon Loaf, we also add pastry cream. And to finish, we sprinkle them with sugar, hazelnuts and chopped chocolate, to give a sweet, rich, crispy stick with bitter notes of cinnamon and dark chocolate.

4 small sticks, each baked in an aluminium foil loaf tin measuring 18 x 7 cm

DOUGH
see ingredients on page 182

BUTTER AND CINNAMON FILLING
see ingredients and method on page 185

PASTRY CREAM
½ vanilla pod
250 g whole milk
70 g sugar
40 g egg yolks (approximately 2 egg yolks)
20 g cornflour

BRUSHING AND SPRINKLING
butter, for greasing
sugar, for sprinkling
80 g hazelnuts
20 g cane (sparkling) sugar
1 egg, beaten
50 g dark chocolate, 85 per cent cocoa solids

PASTRY CREAM
Split the vanilla pod and scrape out the seeds. Place the pod and seeds in a saucepan along with the milk and half the sugar and bring to the boil. Put the remaining sugar in a bowl with the egg yolks and cornflour and stir to combine. Fish out and discard the vanilla pod from the boiling milk. Pour half of the boiling milk mixture into the egg yolk mixture and beat it with a fork. Bring the rest of the milk remaining in the pan back to the boil. Pour the egg yolk and milk mixture into the saucepan while whisking vigorously. Reduce the heat to a simmer as you continue to whisk the mixture for another minute or two. Pour the custard into a large dish and cover directly with clingfilm (this prevents the cream forming a skin). Place the cream in the fridge to cool completely before use.

DOUGH
See pages 173–4 for instructions on how to mix the ingredients and knead the dough before leaving it to rest somewhere cool for 1 hour.

Once the dough is rested, divide it into four equal-sized lumps and shape as follows: roll each lump into a 30 x 15-cm rectangle and turn so the short ends face you. Spread one-quarter of the filling evenly onto each piece. Take the short end of one piece farthest from you and roll the dough towards you like a Swiss roll. Repeat with the remaining dough.

Take four aluminium foil loaf tins and cut them down until their rims are only 1.5 cm high. Butter them generously and sprinkle the insides with sugar. Place one dough sausage into each tin. Use a sharp pair of scissors to cut eight snips almost all the way through the dough at an angle of 45 degrees. Turn and alternate each snip (see photo). Leave the loaves to rise for 1–2 hours as described on page 174.

Meanwhile, add the hazelnuts to a dry, very hot frying pan and toast them for about 5 minutes, or until golden brown. Leave to cool before chopping and adding to the cane (sparkling) sugar. Brush the cinnamon sticks with beaten egg and sprinkle with the nut mixture.

Bake the sticks at 180°C, Gas Mark 4, as per page 175, for about 14 minutes. Transfer the loaves to a rack to cool. Melt the chocolate over a bain marie or in a microwave and drizzle on top.

STICKY CINNAMON BUNS

Cinnamon is a spice I never get tired of. In Denmark we most often use Chinese cinnamon with its strong and distinctive flavour. The milder – and costlier – so-called genuine cinnamon from Ceylon has a more refined and aromatic taste.

10 buns

DOUGH
see ingredients on page 182

BUTTER AND CINNAMON FILLING
see ingredients and method on page 185

BRUSHING AND TOPPING
1 egg, beaten
50 g dark chocolate, melted

DOUGH
See pages 173–4 for instructions on how to mix the ingredients and knead the dough before leaving it somewhere cool for 1 hour.

Once the dough is rested, roll it into a 50 x 20-cm rectangle, and turn it so that its short end faces you. Spread the filling evenly across the dough but leave 5 cm at the short end farthest from you.

Take hold of the short end closest to you and roll the dough away from you into a fat sausage shape. Cut the sausage into 10 equal slices and tuck the 5 cm of bare dough underneath the bun. Arrange the buns on two baking sheets lined with nonstick baking paper. Be sure to leave plenty of space between them.

Leave the sticky buns to rise for 1–2 hours as described on page 174.

Brush the sticky buns with the beaten egg. Bake at 200°C, Gas Mark 6, following the instructions on page 175, for approximately 10 minutes.

Transfer the buns to a rack to cool before drizzling them with the melted chocolate.

CHOCOLATE BUNS

Chocolate Buns are a Danish classic and throughout generations have brought children and adults alike much joy. Stuff the buns with pastry cream and don't be shy when it comes to the dark chocolate, both as an extra filling and on top. You can vary this recipe by using your favourite marmalade as extra filling instead of the chocolate.

10 buns

DOUGH
see ingredients on page 182

PASTRY CREAM
see ingredients and method on page 186

FILLING, BRUSHING, AND TOPPING
100 g plain chocolate, 85 per cent cocoa solids
1 egg, beaten

DOUGH
See pages 173–4 for instructions on how to mix the ingredients and knead the dough before leaving it to rest somewhere cool for 1 hour.

Once the dough is rested, roll it into a 50 x 20-cm rectangle. Use a sharp knife to cut the dough into 10 uniformly sized 10-cm squares. Place a spoonful of pastry cream in the middle of each square. Chop half the chocolate coarsely and scatter a little onto each dollop of pastry cream. Set aside the remaining chocolate for the topping.

Close the buns by grasping each corner and then placing them gently on top of the filling, being careful not to squash it. Arrange the buns seam-side down on two baking sheets lined with nonstick baking paper. Be sure to leave plenty of space between the buns.

Leave the buns to rise for 2–3 hours as described on page 174.

Brush the sticky buns with the beaten egg, then bake at 200°C, Gas Mark 6, following the instructions on page 175, for approximately 10 minutes.

Transfer the buns to a rack and leave to cool before melting the remaining chocolate and spreading it on top.

NORDIC KRINGLE WITH RHUBARB COMPOTE

Here's a classic Nordic type of pretzel just the way our Danish grandmothers made them, and stuffed with a rhubarb compote and marzipan filling. This is a treat that's at its best straight out of the oven. However, in the unlikely event that there are any leftovers, you can always reheat them in the oven and they'll still taste absolutely lovely. You can even freeze any leftovers and then thaw and heat them before serving.

1 pretzel (10 servings)

DOUGH
see ingredients page 182

BUTTER FILLING
200 g salted butter
200 g sugar
200 g marzipan

RHUBARB COMPOTE
500 g rhubarb
250 g sugar
100 g water

BRUSHING AND TOPPING
1 egg, beaten
50 g chopped hazelnuts

FILLING
See method on page 185.

RHUBARB COMPOTE
Wash the rhubarb and chop it into pieces about 1.5 cm in size. Put the rhubarb, sugar and water in a saucepan over a high heat. Bring to the boil, then simmer until the rhubarb pieces turn soft and the compote thickens. Pour into a container with a lid, cover and place in the fridge to cool completely.

DOUGH
See pages 173–4 for instructions on how to mix the ingredients and knead the dough before leaving it to rest somewhere cool for 1 hour.

Once the dough is rested, roll it into an 80 x 20-cm rectangle. Turn it so that the long side is facing you. Place the filling in a line along the middle, then set the rhubarb compote on top of the filling. Then fold one long side over the filling and then the other, ensuring that the dough envelops both filling and rhubarb compote completely.

Carefully press down on the seam then gently turn the dough over so it is now seam-side down. Carefully shape the dough into a figure of eight (see photo).

Leave the dough to rise for 2–3 hours as described on page 174.

Brush with the beaten egg and sprinkle with chopped hazelnuts.

Bake at 180°C, Gas Mark 4, following the instructions on page 175, for about 25 minutes.

#TIP
Try experimenting with different fillings, for example, chopped apples, nuts or raisins. But remember to reduce the amount of compote depending on how juicy your chosen filling is because you don't want it to be too wet.

NORDIC CHRISTMAS CAKE WITH PLUM COMPOTE, CURRANTS AND CARDAMOM

The pleasant fragrance and flavour of cardamom, succulent currants, real butter and a surface as shiny as a mirror will bring Christmas cheer to adults and children alike. If you haven't managed to make your plum compote in time, you can always buy some, or use orange marmalade softened with a little water.

2 cakes

DOUGH
see ingredients on page 182

BUTTER FILLING
100 g salted butter, softened
100 g sugar
100 g marzipan

PLUM COMPOTE
500 g plums, such as Mirabelle, washed and
    pitted
250 g sugar
1 vanilla pod
juice and zest from 1 organic lemon
50 g water

FILLING
5 g ground cardamom
50 g currants

BRUSHING
1 egg, beaten

BUTTER FILLING
See method on page 185.

PLUM COMPOTE
Add all the ingredients to a saucepan over a high heat. Bring to the boil, then let simmer for 30 minutes, or until the compote thickens. Pour the compote into a fine wire sieve balanced over a bowl and leave to drain for about 10 minutes (reserve the syrup for brushing onto the cakes when they come out of the oven). Put the compote in a container with a lid, cover, and place in the fridge to cool completely. Leave the syrup to cool at room temperature.

DOUGH
See pages 173–4 for instructions on how to mix the ingredients and knead the dough before leaving to rest somewhere cool for 1 hour.

Once the dough is rested, chop into two halves and roll each lump into a 25-cm square. Place the butter filling in a long line down the middle and place the plum compote on top of the filling. Sprinkle with cardamom and currants.

Finish the Christmas cakes by first folding each corner over the middle. Then fold 1 cm of the new corners back over themselves again to make sure that the filling stays in. Turn the cakes over so they are now seam-side down, and place on two baking sheets lined with nonstick baking paper. Gently press down on the cakes to level them out. Finally score the dough in the centre of each cake.

Leave the cakes to rise as described on page 174, for approximately 2 hours.

Brush the cakes with the beaten egg and bake at 225°C, Gas Mark 7, for 10 minutes. Then reduce the heat to 200°C, Gas Mark 6, and bake for approximately 10 minutes, or until the cakes are wonderfully golden in colour.

Remove the cakes from the oven and brush them with the reserved plum syrup, then transfer to a rack to cool.

#TIP
If your plum syrup has thickened so much that it's no longer easy to brush on to the cake, heat it a little to thin it down until it is a good consistency for brushing.

CINNAMON SWIRLS

This recipe for Cinnamon Swirls was given to me by Morten Schakenda, a Norwegian from the bakery in Lom. After sampling these wonderful swirls at a food conference, the taste of cinnamon is forever linked in my mind with Schakenda's swirls. My numerous attempts at recreating these didn't work out, and so finally, we had to take a trip into the Norwegian wilderness to bring his recipe back to Meyer's Bakeries.

Approximately 12 swirls

DOUGH
500 g cold whole milk
50 g fresh organic baking yeast
1 egg
1 kg plain flour
150 g sugar
10 g salt
15 g ground cardamom
150 g salted butter, cold

BUTTER AND CINNAMON FILLING
see ingredients and method on page 185

BRUSHING
1 egg, beaten

DOUGH
See pages 200–3 for information on how to mix the ingredients, knead the dough and shape it into Cinnamon Swirls. (Refer to page 174 if you plan to knead the dough by hand.)

Let the Cinnamon Swirls rise for 1–2 hours as described on page 174.

Brush the swirls with beaten egg, then bake the swirls at 200°C, Gas Mark 6, following the instructions on page 175, for approximately 10–15 minutes. Transfer to a rack to cool.

#TIP
Try using coarse dark brown sugar instead of white sugar to give your swirls a deeper flavour.

#TIP
If you're making a huge portion of Cinnamon Swirls for a festive occasion, you can knead and shape the swirls the day before and then leave them in the fridge overnight. When you are ready to bake, remove them from the fridge and leave to rise to completion at room temperature before putting them in the oven. If you want to be prepared even further ahead of the festivities or simply want to stock up, you can also freeze unbaked Cinnamon Swirls. See page 175 for thawing and baking instructions.

HOW TO MAKE THE DOUGH AND SHAPE THE CINNAMON SWIRLS

1. Pour the milk into a the bowl of a food stand mixer and add the fresh yeast.

2. Stir well until the yeast dissolves completely.

3. Mix in the egg and then add all the dry ingredients. Attach the dough hook to the mixer and knead on low speed for approximately 8 minutes, or until the dough is shiny and firm.

4. Add lumps of cold butter into the bowl.

5. Mix again on low speed for approximately 8 minutes, or until the butter is completely absorbed and the dough is shiny and firm once again.

6. Sprinkle your work surface generously with flour and tip the dough out onto it. Roll it into a 60 x 30-cm rectangle.

7. Spread the butter filling evenly across the entire surface of the dough.

8. Starting from one of the short ends, fold one-third of the dough across the middle. Make three layers by folding the remaining one-third over the folded third.

9. Roll the dough into a 30-cm square about 1.5 cm thick.

10. Cut the square into strips about 2.5 cm wide and 30 cm long.

11. Take one strip and place it in front of you.

12. Hold on to one end with one hand while using your other to roll or twist the other end of the strip, working towards yourself. You need to twist the dough 6 or 7 times in total.

13. Pick up the twirled strip of dough with both hands and twist it twice around the index and middle finger on one hand, ensuring a little still hangs loose.

14. Place the overhanging piece of dough (the end) across both swirls and place it between your index and middle finger.

15. Pull your fingers back, thus pulling the end into the swirl and fastening it there.

16. Arrange the finished cinnamon swirls with plenty of space between them on two nonstick baking sheets.

BLUEBERRY SWIRLS

Blueberries impart pastries with a lovely flavour, so try this alternative to the Cinnamon Swirl when blueberries are in season. These swirls are hugely successful in our bakeries.

Approximately 12 swirls

DOUGH
see ingredients on page 199

BLUEBERRY SYRUP
500 g frozen blueberries
200 g cane sugar
½ vanilla pod

LIGHT BUTTER FILLING
150 g salted butter, softened
150 g marzipan
150 g cane sugar

BLUEBERRY SYRUP
Add the frozen blueberries to a small flameproof oven dish, sprinkle evenly with the sugar, and bake at 200°C, Gas Mark 6, for 25 minutes. Move them around a little after 10 minutes to ensure that they're baking evenly.

Pour the blueberries into a sieve set over a saucepan and leave to drain for 20 minutes. Transfer the berries to a bowl and leave them somewhere cool. Add the vanilla pod to the blueberry juice in the saucepan and place over a high heat. Bring to the boil and reduce until thick. Once the syrup reaches 100°C, remove from the heat and leave to cool.

LIGHT BUTTER FILLING
While the syrup is cooling, make the light butter filling following the instructions on page 185. Mix the cooled syrup with the light butter filling to make a light blueberry and butter filling.

DOUGH
See pages 200–3 for information on how to make the dough and shape the swirls, but this time use the blueberry filling instead of the cinnamon filling. Sprinkle the reserved berries on top of the filling before you fold the dough.

Let the swirls rise for 1–2 hours as described on page 174.

Bake the swirls at 200°C, Gas Mark 6, following the instructions on page 175, for approximately 10–15 minutes. Transfer to a rack to cool.

AMBROSIA CUBE CAKES

Ambrosia was the name given to the food that rendered the mythological gods of Ancient Greece immortal and eternally youthful. We can't promise you as much, but we can offer you this recipe. If you don't want to make your own marmalade, buy a good-quality orange marmalade instead.

12 cube cakes

DOUGH
see ingredients on page 199

ORANGE MARMALADE
300 g organic oranges
150 g cane sugar
1 vanilla pod

MARZIPAN AND DATE MIXTURE
100 g marzipan
100 g pitted dates

BRUSHING AND TOPPING
1 egg, beaten
icing sugar, for dusting

ORANGE MARMALADE
Wash the oranges, cut them into 1-cm cubes, and add them to a saucepan over a high heat. Pour in cold water to cover and bring to the boil. Reduce the heat and simmer for 1 minute. Transfer the orange mixture to a sieve set over a bowl and leave to drain. Return the oranges to the saucepan, add the sugar and seeds from the vanilla pod, and slowly bring to 110°C over a low heat (this should take about 30 minutes).

Once they have caramelized, set the oranges aside to cool completely before adding them to the dough.

MARZIPAN AND DATE MIXTURE
Use a large knife to chop the marzipan and dates roughly. Mix them together well to ensure you get a little of both with every bite of the finished cube cakes.

DOUGH
See page 200 for instructions on how to mix the ingredients and knead the dough before letting it rest somewhere cool for 1 hour.

Shape the Ambrosia Cube Cakes as described on pages 208–9.

Let the cakes rise for 1–2 hours as described on page 174.

Brush the cakes with beaten egg, then bake at 200°C, Gas Mark 6, following the instructions on page 175, for approximately 10–15 minutes. Transfer to a rack to cool.

Brush the cakes with any leftover orange syrup and dust with icing sugar to finish.

1. Roll the dough into a
30 x 40-cm rectangle.

HOW TO SHAPE AMBROSIA CUBE CAKES

2. Brush some of the beaten egg all over the surface of the dough. Cover the surface with an even layer of caramelized oranges followed by the marzipan and date mixture (save a little of the orange syrup for brushing the baked cakes).

3. Roll the dough towards you like a Swiss roll, then brush the surface with some more beaten egg. Using a large knife or dough scraper, cut the roll into slices about 1 cm thick.

4. Chop the slices into 1-cm cubes.

5. Line 1 or 2 baking sheets with nonstick baking paper. Gently arrange the little cubes together to make 12 cakes, but make sure you don't squeeze the cubes too hard. Leave plenty of space between the cube cakes.

BURGER BUNS

Baking your own burger buns is really easy but beware! Once you and your kids have tried these succulent, soft, tasty and absolutely additive-free buns, the ready-made kind, or the type served in fast food restaurants, will never taste the same again.

15 buns

DOUGH
350 g cold water
15 g fresh organic baking yeast
2 eggs
630 g plain flour
70 g whole-grain heritage or regular whole-grain wheat flour
55 g sugar
10 g salt
90 g salted butter, softened

BRUSHING AND SPRINKLING
1 egg, beaten
sesame seeds

See pages 173–4 for instructions on how to mix the ingredients and knead the dough before leaving it rest for 1 hour.

Once the dough is rested, divide into 15 equal lumps and shape them into buns. Arrange them, spaced well apart, on three baking sheets lined with nonstick baking paper. Place another piece of paper on top of the buns and press down on the buns until they are approximately 1 cm in height.

Let the buns rise for 2–3 hours as described on page 174.

Brush the buns with beaten egg and sprinkle with the sesame seeds.

Bake at 220°C, Gas Mark 7, following the instructions on page 175, for approximately 12 minutes. Transfer to a rack to cool.

HOT-DOG BUNS

Most of the kids I know – and their parents for that matter – love hot dogs. And if you make the buns yourself, buy high-quality frankfurters and serve them with a lovely salad, it quickly turns into a nutritious and filling meal.

12 buns

DOUGH
250 g cold water
15 g fresh organic baking yeast
1 egg
500 g plain flour
45 g sugar
5 g salt
40 g salted butter, softened

See pages 173–4 for instructions on how to mix the ingredients and knead the dough before leaving it to rest somewhere nice and warm for 15–20 minutes.

Once the dough is rested, divide it into 12 equally sized lumps, and shape and roll them into elongated hot-dog buns. Arrange them spaced well apart on 2 baking sheets lined with nonstick baking paper and leave to rise until doubled in size (see page 174).

Bake the hot-dog buns at 180°C, Gas Mark 4, following the instructions on page 175, for approximately 12–14 minutes. Remove the buns from the oven while they're still only light brown on top and transfer to a rack to cool. Reheat the buns before serving.

WHEAT CARDAMOM BUNS

In Denmark there is a festival known as Great Prayer Day, which falls on the fourth Sunday after Easter. When the holiday was put on the statute books in 1686, all work and trades, including baking, were forbidden from sundown the day before Great Prayer Day and on the day itself. To get around the law, Danish bakers made a type of wheat bun that people could take home and heat up the following day. More often than not, people ate the buns while they were still warm and crisp, so eating the buns the night before Great Prayer Day became a Danish tradition. However, there's no law to stop you from enjoying these buns at any time of the year.

15 buns

DOUGH
15 g fresh organic baking yeast
175 g cold water
175 g cold whole milk
2 eggs
700 g plain flour
55 g sugar
10 g ground cardamom
10 g salt
55 g salted butter, softened

See pages 173–4 for instructions on how to mix the ingredients and knead the dough before leaving it to rest.

Once the dough is rested, divide it into 15 equally sized lumps.

Shape the buns by placing a piece of dough in the palm of one hand and rolling it around with the palm of your other hand.

Arrange the buns in a roasting tin lined with nonstick baking paper, leaving 5 cm between each bun.

Let the buns rise for 2–3 hours as described on page 174. Once the buns have risen to double their original size, they'll touch one another, and this will give them the proper wheat bun shape.

Bake the buns at 180°C, Gas Mark 4, following the instructions on page 175, for approximately 15–20 minutes. Transfer to a rack to cool.

CARROT BUNS

A delicious, soft bun enhanced with colour from the carrots and crunchiness from the sunflower seeds. Kids love these buns and happily devour them as a snack or as part of a packed lunch.

12 buns

DOUGH
50 g fresh organic baking yeast
500 g cold water
1 kg plain flour
75 g sugar
15 g salt
100 g salted butter, softened

FILLING
2 eggs
150 g sunflower seeds
4 large carrots, peeled and finely grated

See pages 173–4 for instructions on how to mix the ingredients and knead the dough before leaving it to rest.

Once the dough is rested, sprinkle your work surface with flour and tip the dough out onto it. Make a well in the centre of the dough and pour the eggs, sunflower seeds and grated carrots into it. Incorporate the ingredients by folding the dough into a huge bun then chop it into small pieces using a knife, being sure to mix in the eggs. The dough doesn't have to be completely evenly kneaded, but it should be smooth.

Divide the dough into 12 equally sized buns (a little like burger buns) and gently arrange them, spaced well apart, on one or two baking sheets lined with nonstick baking paper.

Let the buns rise for 1–2 hours as described on page 174.

Bake the carrot buns at 220°C, Gas Mark 7 following the instructions on page 175, for about 15 minutes. Transfer to a rack to cool.

WHAT'S WRONG WITH MY ENRICHED DOUGH – AND HOW DO I FIX IT?

Things don't always go according to plan when baking with enriched dough, so we've provided you with a guide to some of the most common problems you may encounter. Use this guide to try and solve the problems as they arise or next time around.

Remember that there may be several reasons for the same problem and sometimes there might even be directly opposing reasons behind it. When this happens, you'll need to consider what factor is most likely to have caused your specific problem or try to correct several things all at once.

MY DOUGH IS TOO DENSE

You've over-kneaded your dough

Lower the speed of the food stand mixer or don't knead your dough for quite as long. If your dough loses its toughness, you've over-kneaded it and the gluten strands have been stretched to the extent that they can no longer contract. If you plan to knead dough for a long time, it's important that the ingredients are cold from the start. This will keep the temperature from rising too much during kneading.

If you sense that your dough is getting a little too warm as you are kneading it, place the mixing bowl in the fridge to lower the temperature.

The dough has not risen sufficiently

Let your dough rise for longer the next time around. This will make it lighter and more porous.

BUTTER LEAKS OUT OF MY DOUGH WHEN RISING/BAKING

The dough has risen in surroundings that are too warm

If your surroundings are too warm the butter will melt and leak out of the dough during rising. In addition, if the butter is not fully absorbed in the dough it may leak out while baking. Make sure the dough is left to rise in a place where the temperature is consistent. When baking, never set enriched dough on a preheated hot baking sheet.

If you do get a sense that the surroundings are too warm to let your dough rise, place the baking sheet in the fridge while the dough rises.

The dough has over-risen

If you leave the dough for too long at room temperature and the butter is on the brink of melting, it may separate while baking. Make sure the butter isn't too soft or warm when you use it, and knead it all in at once. Don't leave your dough to rise for as long next time. You can also add a little extra yeast to your dough if you plan to leave it to rise somewhere cool, but if you add too much yeast, your dough will taste of alcohol.

MY DOUGH COLLAPSES BEFORE BAKING

The dough has over-risen

The longer your dough rises, the more fragile its gluten strands. You brush most types of pastry dough with egg before baking, and this will often cause the dough to collapse if it's been left to rise for too long. Next time shorten the rising time, leave it in a cooler place, and keep an eye on the dough rather than on your watch.

If you notice that your pastry dough is rising a little too quickly, for example in the heat of summer, trust your senses and slide it into the oven as soon as you think it has risen enough.

OTHER BAKED GOODS

At Meyer's Bakeries we bake lots of goodies that don't really belong in any of the chapters on wheat bread, whole-grain bread, rye bread or pastries. However, we would feel dishonest if we didn't share these recipes as well. So here are some types of bread made with alternative types of natural starters. You will also find recipes for snack-breads, pizza crusts and crunchy things such as crispbread and biscuits. And to top it all off we include recipes for our highly popular Gingerbread Hearts and classic English Scones.

EVERYDAY WHEAT LOAF

This is actually the bread I bake most often, which is practically every day. I use a pre-fermentation method where I take one-third of the dough I've just made to use in a fresh batch of dough. I'll knead this dough while the first batch is in the oven. In other words, I end up with freshly baked bread as well as dough ready for baking the following day. You can go freestyle a little in terms of overall amounts of flour, and you can even add a little more whole-grain flour if you like. Occasionally, if you get the feeling that your dough is losing its rising power, simply add a little baking yeast to stimulate the dough back into action.

1 loaf of bread and pre-fermentation for your next batch

PRE-FERMENT
200 g water
5 g fresh organic baking yeast
125 g bread flour
125 g rye flour
1½ teaspoons honey

DOUGH
1 portion of pre-ferment
600 g cold water
20 g salt
200 g stone-milled whole-grain wheat flour
650 g bread flour, divided

PRE-FERMENT
Add the water and yeast to a bowl and stir until the yeast has dissolved. Then add the remaining ingredients and mix well. Cover and set aside to ferment at room temperature for 2–3 days.

DOUGH
Put the pre-ferment dough into a large mixing bowl. Add the water, salt and the whole-grain flour along with half of the regular bread flour and beat everything together with a wooden spoon. Continue to mix thoroughly but lift and stretch the dough with your spoon to get as much air into it as possible (this will make the dough tougher).

Add as much of the wheat flour as the dough will hold. This step should take 5–6 minutes, but if you have the muscle power, carry on for another 5–10 minutes – the tougher your gluten structure, the easier it will be for your dough to rise. You can also knead the dough at intervals by working the dough for 3–4 minutes and then taking a 5-minute break; repeating 3 times in all. Taking breaks like this allows the flour to absorb all the liquid and you won't have to work as hard. Cover the dough with a dampened clean tea towel or clingfilm and let it rise overnight in the fridge. When the dough has risen by about two-thirds its original size, it's ready for the oven.

Place a baking stone or pizza stone in the oven and preheat to 275°C, Gas Mark 10. Sprinkle your work surface with flour and carefully tip the dough onto it. Take one-third of the dough and set aside – this will be your pre-ferment for your next batch of dough. Using the dough on your work surface, tighten its surface as described on page 60.

Bake the bread as described on pages 60–1, for approximately 40 minutes. If the crust turns too dark during baking, cover it with aluminium foil.

PRE-FERMENT FOR THE NEXT BATCH
Now prepare the dough you set aside. Ideally, you should bake this dough within 24 hours. If this is not possible, it can be kept in the fridge for up to 2 days. Follow the same procedure as above. This way, you have a fresh batch of dough ready for the oven the following day.

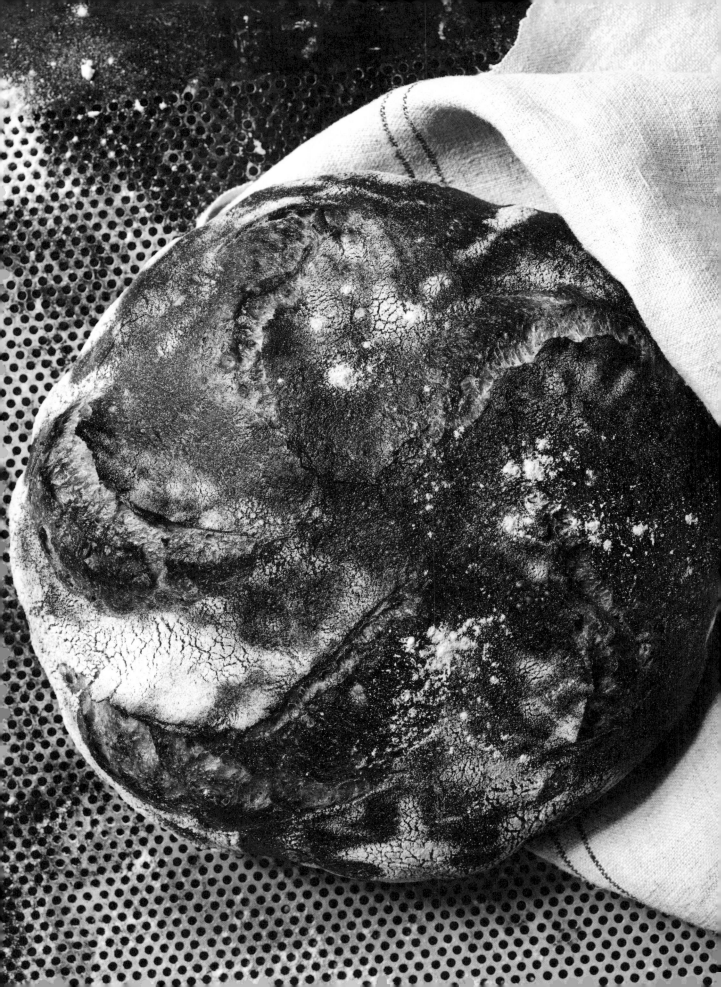

GRANTOFTEGAARD BREAD

This bread is named after Grantoftegaard, the organic farm in Ballerup, in Denmark, where we buy a lot of the grain we use in our organic wheat flour. It's a slightly more advanced recipe, because we use only a natural starter as a rising agent, and no baking yeast at all. So, to enhance the rising power of our natural starter, it must be thicker than our regular wheat starter and be happily bubbling away before being added to the dough. This particular bread is greatly inspired by Chad Robertson from San Francisco, who's visited a few times and also taught courses at Meyer's Madhus.

1 loaf

PRE-FERMENT
2 teaspoons basic natural starter (see page 230)
100 g lukewarm water
50 g whole-grain wheat flour
50 g bread flour

DOUGH
100 g pre-ferment
450 g lukewarm water
100 g whole-grain wheat flour
500 g bread flour
15 g salt

SHAPING
50 g rice flour
50 g bread flour

PRE-FERMENT
Mix the basic natural starter with the water and the two types of wheat flour until it almost has a consistency like porridge. Use your hands by all means. Leave it in the warmest spot in your home, optimally at 25–28°C for 6–8 hours, or until it's risen by 20–30 per cent. The texture should be light and frothy and the fragrance sweet and floury.

You only need to use 100 g of this pre-ferment in the dough, so reserve the rest and use it as a basic natural starter the next time you want to bake Grantoftegaard bread. (Remember to feed the pre-ferment occasionally.)

Method continued overleaf...

#TIP
You can test whether or not your pre-ferment is ready by adding 1 tablespoon of pre-ferment to a small bowl of water. If the fermentation floats, it's ready for use. If it sinks to the bottom, leave it a little longer and test it again.

HOW TO MAKE A BASIC NATURAL STARTER

If you have some starter that's in good shape, for example, a wheat stock starter (see page 40), use this as the preliminary starter in your basic starter. However, you will need to refresh it for three days, before it's ready for use in the pre-ferment.

FIRST REFRESHING

100 g preliminary starter, such as wheat stock starter or any other natural starter you can get your hands on
50 g cold water
50 g wheat flour
50 g whole-grain wheat flour

SECOND AND THIRD REFRESHING

50 g basic starter
100 g water
50 g wheat flour
50 g whole-grain wheat flour

Mix all the ingredients for the first refreshing in a bowl and leave at room temperature for 24 hours. This mixture is the foundation of your basic starter. Refresh for the second and third time using the quantities stated and leave for 24 hours each time.

Once your natural starter rises and falls again within 24 hours, it's ready for use. If it's not ready after being refreshed a third time, refresh it one more time. If this doesn't help, and the starter you used right at the beginning was not good enough you may have to begin again with another stock starter.

If you bake bread every day or every other day, you can leave the starter at room temperature and then just refresh it by using the quantities stated in the second and third refreshing. If you don't bake that regularly, store the starter in the fridge and then use it as your preliminary starter for your basic starter next time you want to bake Grantoftegaard bread.

DOUGH

See pages 55–9 for instructions on how to mix the dough before leaving it to rest.

Once the dough is rested, tip it out on to your work surface. Tighten the surface of the dough using a dough scraper to push its sides under it, and then shape it into a round loaf (see page 63). Leave to rest for another 30 minutes.

Mix the rice and bread flours together then rub most of it onto a clean tea towel. Place the cloth floury-side up in a proving basket or a bowl slightly smaller in diameter than the cast iron flameproof dish you intend to bake the bread in, with plenty of cloth hanging over the sides. Tighten the dough again and sprinkle the remaining flour mixture on top. Place the dough seam-side up in the proving basket or bowl, and cover it with the overhanging tea towel. Leave to rest in the fridge for 12–24 hours.

Take the dough out of the fridge 1 hour before baking.

Place a cast iron dish, such as a cassserole, covered with its lid, into the oven. Heat the oven to its highest temperature. Once it reaches the hottest temperature, wearing thick oven gloves, carefully take the very hot casserole and its lid out of the oven. Warning: both the pot and the lid will be very, very hot. Remove the lid and set it somewhere safe on the stove. Carefully place the dough in the saucepan, cover with the hot lid and return to the oven. After 10 minutes turn the temperature down to 230°C, Gas Mark 8, and leave to bake for another 5 minutes. Wearing oven gloves, remove the hot lid and bake the bread for another 30–35 minutes until the loaf sounds hollow when you tap it and it's turned dark brown. You can also measure the core temperature by inserting the probe of a kitchen thermometer into the centre of the loaf. When the temperature reaches 98–100°C°, the bread is done.

#NOTE

Make sure that every part of your casserole is heatproof and that there are no plastic knobs on the lid that could melt.

LEVAIN BREAD

Levain is actually just the French word for starter, but it is also the name for a specific type of natural starter based on the wild yeast cells that develop when you ferment dried fruit, in this case raisins. It takes eight days to prepare levain for use, but you end up with a wonderfully fresh starter that's so powerful there's no need to add baking yeast.

4 small loaves

START-UP LEVAIN
15 organic raisins
300 g cold water

LEVAIN STARTER
150 g start-up levain
90 g bread flour

REFRESHING LEVAIN STARTER
150 g levain starter
150 g cold water
90 g bread flour

DOUGH
650 g cold water
300 g levain starter
900 g bread flour
100 g heritage bread flour
30 g salt

START-UP LEVAIN
Put the raisins in a container and pour the water over them. Place a lid on top and leave for 5 days at room temperature. Drain and discard the raisins. Your start-up levain is ready for use.

LEVAIN STARTER
Once you mix your start-up levain with bread flour you have a levain starter. Leave at room temperature loosely sealed with a lid or draped with clingfilm for 3 days and give it a good stir every day.

REFRESHING LEVAIN STARTER
Refresh your levain starter by taking 150 g of the levain starter and mixing in the cold water and bread flour. Cover the mixture loosely with a lid or drape it with clingfilm and leave for 12 hours at room temperature.

DOUGH
Add the water, levain starter and both types of wheat flour to a food stand mixer bowl. Attach the dough hook and knead slowly for 5 minutes. Increase the speed and knead for 6 minutes. Add salt to the dough and knead for another minute at the highest speed. Pour the dough into a greased, lidded container, cover and leave to rise in the fridge for at least 12 hours.

Take the dough out of the fridge and leave at room temperature for about 1 hour. Sprinkle your work surface with flour then tip the dough out onto it. Cut the dough into four equally sized lumps. Roll the lumps into balls and leave them to rest for 5 minutes before rolling into sausages. Place the dough in four separate proving baskets sprinkled with flour. (Or you can place them on a baking sheet lined with nonstick baking paper). Leave the dough to rise for 1½ hours at room temperature.

Meanwhile, place a baking stone or pizza stone in the oven and preheat the oven to 250°C, Gas Mark 9. When hot, carefully place the dough loaves on a piece of nonstick baking paper (if you've used proving baskets), score them with a sharp knife and push them onto the baking stone using the paper. Bake for 20–25 minutes, or until their crust turns a lovely dark colour and becomes crisp.

WHEAT BREAD WITH APPLE 'STARTER'

This is on my personal top-five list of favourite breads; it's baked with Øland, my favourite wheat grain, but you can use any heritage wheat you like in this recipe. Here we use apples as the leavening agent. The yeast in fruit provides a somewhat milder starter and it also imparts a little sweetness. It takes 5–6 days before the apple starter is ready for use. Apple starter will often oxidize, which yields very handsome and dark loaves. If you're not quite convinced that your apple starter is strong enough, you can always add 1.5 grams instant yeast to your dough. Then you can rest assured that the dough will rise, and you'll still get that lovely sour and fruity taste from the apple starter.

1 large loaf or 2 smaller ones

APPLE STARTER
200 g ripe organic apples

DOUGH
100 g Apple Starter
500 g water
450 g bread flour
150 g heritage whole-grain wheat flour
or 150 g rye flour
15 g salt

APPLE STARTER
Wash and core the apples and blend (with their skin) in a food processor until mashed. Pour the mashed apples into a glass jar with a loose-fitting lid that will allow any gases produced to escape easily (see warning on page 41). Leave to ferment at room temperature for 7 days.

Do not let it stand somewhere too warm or it may start to become mouldy.

Give it a stir once a day. Once the starter begins to smell like dark beer it is ready to use.

DOUGH
See pages 55–60 for information on how to combine the ingredients and mix the dough before leaving it to rest.

Leave the dough to rise and then bake following the instructions on pages 63.

#TIP
You can keep the leftover apple starter in the fridge for the next time you want to bake this type of bread, but if it becomes mouldy, put it in the bin. If it stays fresh, simply mix the old mashed apples with the freshly mashed apples in a ratio of 1:4 and leave at room temperature. It should be ready for use after only 3–4 days.

HUNGARIAN POTATO BREAD

The recipe for these deep-fried flatbreads can be traced all the way back to Roman times. Today they're a highly popular street food in both Hungary and Austria. You can enjoy them with all sorts of toppings or as a side dish with a salad or stew.

16 flatbreads

DOUGH
50 g wheat stock starter (see page 40)
250 g water
15 g fresh organic baking yeast
400 g bread flour
200 g whole-grain heritage or
    regular bread flour
400 g scrubbed potatoes, cooked, peeled and
    cut into 1-cm cubes
20 g salt
neutral oil, for frying

See pages 55–60 for information on how to combine the ingredients and mix the dough before you leave it to rise.

Tip the dough out onto your work surface as soon as it's finished rising. Cut or chop the dough into 16 equally sized lumps and flatten them with your hands. If the dough sticks to either your hands or the table, sprinkle it with a little flour. Pour 1-cm of oil into a deep frying pan and heat until it reaches around 140°C. Add a couple of flat pieces of dough to the hot oil and fry for approximately 4 minutes on each side.

Transfer the finished flatbreads to a dish lined with kitchen paper while you fry the rest. Leave the flatbreads to cool before serving.

CRISP PIZZA

Meyer's Bakeries' pizzas are extremely popular and this is our recipe for a heavenly crisp pizza crust. In our bakeries, we scatter grated cheese and chopped asparagus on the dough before baking it, and then added slices of cured ham on top. Of course, you can vary the toppings with any of your favourite combinations.

6 pizzas

DOUGH
3 g fresh organic baking yeast
   or 1 g instant yeast
550 g cold water
800 g bread flour
200g heritage wheat flour
25 g salt

Add the water and yeast to the bowl of a stand mixer and stir until the yeast dissolves. Add the flours and attach the dough hook to the mixer. Set the machine to low speed and knead the dough for 4 minutes. Add the salt and knead for another minute. Oil your work surface, tip the dough out onto the oil, and roll it around to cover all sides. Leave the dough to rest for 20 minutes.

Cut or chop the dough into 6 equally sized lumps and roll them into balls before placing them on a baking sheet. Cover loosely with clingfilm and leave to rise at room temperature for 2 hours. Then place them in the fridge to continue to rise for 6–12 hours.

Place a pizza stone in the oven and preheat the oven to its highest temperature, at least 30 minutes before you want to cook.

Shape the dough as described below and, if you want to try our version, scatter with grated cheese and chopped asparagus. Slide the pizzas onto the baking stone, one at a time, and bake for 10–14 minutes, or until they're crisp and beautifully dark. Arrange slices of cured ham on top before serving.

HOW TO MAKE A PIZZA

1. Take a ball of dough from the fridge and cover it in flour.

2. First shape the rim with your fingers. Then place the dough on a work surface sprinkled with a little flour. Squeeze the dough into a pizza shape.

3. Hold down the dough with one hand while stretching it with the other. Turn the dough and continue to stretch all the way round.

4. Continue until it's perfectly circular and it is no longer possible to stretch the dough any further. Add your choice of topping. (Here, we've used tomato sauce and grated cheese).

NAAN BREAD

Naan is the Persian word for bread and traditionally, these flat, soft wheat breads are baked in a clay oven, known as a tandoor. You can, however, also cook them in a frying pan or on a baking stone in an oven. This bread is naturally suited to Indian and Pakistani food, but it's equally delicious in a packed lunch or enjoyed as a quick snack.

20 pieces of naan bread

1 kg self-raising flour
200 g milk
1 egg
50 g sugar
25 g salt
50 g rapeseed oil
400 g water
30 g nigella seeds

Place all the ingredients in a large bowl and mix until smooth. If you are using a food stand mixer fitted with a dough hook this takes approximately 5 minutes with the machine set on low speed. Cover the dough loosely with clingfilm and leave to rest for 20 minutes at room temperature.

Divide the dough into 20 equally sized lumps and roll them into small balls. Re-cover the dough balls with the clingfilm and leave to rest at room temperature. After 25 minutes discard the clingfilm and flatten the balls with your hands until they are a couple of millimetres thick, then sprinkle with the nigella seeds.

Place a pizza stone in the oven and preheat the oven to 250°C, Gas Mark 9. Working in batches, slide a few pieces of naan dough onto the pizza stone and bake until crisp on the outside and soft on the inside. The baking time will depend on how hot your oven is, so keep an eye on them and expect them to be done after 4–5 minutes.

#TIP
You can also cook naan bread, a few pieces at a time, in a large, dry, very hot frying pan until they are crisp on the outside and soft on the inside. Depending on how hot the pan is, cooking time can range from 30 seconds to 3 minutes on each side.

CRISPBREAD

Making your own crispbread is not at all difficult and the homemade, crisp variety goes equally well with cheese, cold cuts or marmalade. You can also use these crispbreads as croutons in salads or serve them with your favourite dips.

1 to 2 sheets

DOUGH
2 tablespoons wheat stock starter (see page 40)
400 g cold water
550 g plain flour
85 g rye flour
125 g Øland or other heritage flour
15 g salt

SPRINKLING
55 g mixed flakes, such as rye,
   heritage wheat, oat and emmer

DOUGH
Add all ingredients to a bowl with a lid and mix until smooth and even. Cover the container with the lid, transfer the dough to the fridge for a couple of hours.

Sprinkle your work surface with flour, tip the dough onto it, and flatten it a little with your hands. Dust a large piece of nonstick baking paper with flour and set the flattened dough onto it. Sprinkle another large piece with flour and place it, flour-side down, onto the dough. Roll the dough until it's a couple of millimetres thick then peel off the top layer of paper. Place the dough on its paper onto a baking sheet. Brush the dough with water and sprinkle with the mixed flakes.

Bake the crispbread at 180°C, Gas Mark 4, until crisp, for approximately 10–12 minutes. Leave to cool on a rack. Break into smaller pieces. This will keep for approximately 1 month sealed in an airtight container.

OAT BISCUITS

These oat biscuits have a little more personality because their crunch is very delicate and the cane sugar imparts a subtle fruitiness. You can enjoy them spread with cold butter and some blackberry jam but they also go well with savoury foods, such as a piece of mature Cheddar cheese and a glass of red wine, or simply eat them on their own. This recipe calls for potash, an ingredient that is also used regularly in German baking (so it may be labelled 'pottasche' in German or 'potaske' in Danish). If you cannot find it at your local baking suppliers or a German or Danish deli, you can order it online from www.thegermanbakery.co.uk, or www.germandeli.co.uk.

Approximately 30 biscuits

DOUGH
250 g butter, softened
200 g coarse cane sugar
5 g potash (see above for more details on where to find this ingredient, or see tip)
50 g cold milk
1 egg
3 g salt
250 g coarsely rolled oats
340 g plain flour

Cream the butter and sugar together in a bowl. Dissolve the potash in the milk and stir until smooth. Add the milk, egg, salt, oats and wheat flour into the butter and sugar mixture, then stir and mix to form biscuit dough. Make sure you don't overwork the dough as this might make the biscuits spread while baking. Seal the dough in a resealable food bag or a plastic container with a lid, or seal it in a piece of clingfilm. Leave to rest in the fridge for at least 30 minutes.

Sprinkle your work surface with flour, tip the dough out onto it and flatten it a little with your hands. Then place the dough between two large pieces of nonstick baking paper that have also been dusted with flour. Roll the dough until it's 5 millimetres thick and then peel off the top layer of paper (but don't put it in the bin).

If you like, you can now slide the whole piece of dough and baking paper onto a baking stone or baking sheet. Bake it in one piece at 180°C, Gas Mark 4, until golden, for approximately 15 minutes, then break it into smaller pieces once it's done. Or, you could use a round cutter to cut out shapes and transfer them to the piece of parchment that you peeled off the dough. Slide the paper with the shaped biscuit dough onto the baking stone or baking sheet and bake as above. When they are golden, leave the biscuits to cool on a rack.

#TIP
You can use bicarbonate of soda instead of the potash, but the finished biscuits will just be slightly less crisp.

RYE CRACKERS WITH ROASTED CARAWAY SEEDS

Crisp rye crackers spiced with roasted caraway seeds are perfect with blue cheese or simply spread with a layer of cold butter. If you store the crackers in an airtight container they should keep for up to a month, though chances are they'll never last that long!

Approximately 35 crackers

DOUGH
100 g salted butter
100 g cold milk
20 g caraway seeds
100 g rye flour
100 g heritage wheat flour
3 g baking powder
3 g salt

Melt the butter in a saucepan over a medium heat and then add the cold milk. Meanwhile, in a dry, hot frying pan, roast the caraway seeds for a few minutes, or until they give off a scent. Mix together the rye flour and the heritage wheat flour, baking powder, salt and roasted caraway seeds in a bowl then stir in the butter and milk mixture. Tip the dough out onto your work surface and knead well (you can add more heritage wheat if the dough is a little too soft). Knead until smooth then seal the dough in a resealable food bag or a lidded plastic container ,or seal it in a piece of clingfilm. Then leave it to rest in the fridge for about 2 hours.

Sprinkle flour onto your work surface, tip the dough out onto it and flatten it a little with your hands. Place the dough between two pieces of nonstick baking paper that have also been sprinkled with flour. Roll the dough until it's a few millimetres thick and then peel off the top layer of paper (but don't put it in the bin). Cut the dough into 3 x 6 cm rectangles and place them on the piece of paper you just peeled off of the dough.

Place the paper with the crackers onto a baking sheet and bake at 180°C, Gas Mark 4, until golden, for about 8 minutes. Transfer the crackers to a rack and leave to cool.

#TIP
Instead of simply melting the butter, you can give the crackers a delicate nutty flavour by browning the butter and pouring it through a fine wire sieve into a bowl to remove any sediment. Then add the milk and continue as above.

GINGERBREAD HEARTS

At our bakery, the pre-dough is made in early November, and then kept in a kitchen cupboard for a month to improve the flavour of the gingerbread. You can make the dough right away if you're in a hurry – the flavour won't be as intense, but it will still be delicious. Baking the hearts in early December means they'll keep, stored in the fridge, until Christmas – if they're not eaten before then!

Approximately 20 hearts

PRE-DOUGH
500 g honey
250 g plain flour

GINGERBREAD DOUGH
2 egg yolks
10 g baker's ammonia
10 g potash (see page 249)
750 g pre-dough
250 g plain flour
5 g ground cinnamon
5 g ground ginger
5 g ground cloves
oil, for greasing
flour, for sprinkling

COATING
200 g plain chocolate, preferably 85 per cent cocoa solids, melted

PRE-DOUGH
Heat the honey until it reaches 40–50°C. Add the honey and flour to a bowl and work them well together with your hands. Pour the mixture into a container and seal with a lid. Store the pre-dough somewhere not too hot, such as a kitchen cupboard, for at least one month. Please note that the pre-dough may turn hard – even rock-hard – but that's OK. When the potash is added, a chemical reaction takes place that slowly softens the dough.

GINGERBREAD DOUGH
Add the egg yolks and baker's ammonia to a bowl and mix together until smooth. Then add potash to one or two spoonfuls of milk or water (be careful as it may get hot). Add the egg yolk and potash mixture to the pre-dough along with the flour, cinnamon, ginger and cloves and knead well. (If you've not made a pre-dough in advance, add the ingredients for the pre-dough now). By hand this will take 6–8 minutes but in a stand mixer fitted with the dough hook, allow 3 minutes at low speed and then 3 minutes at full speed.

Grease a nonstick baking sheet with a little oil, dust with flour and set aside. Preheat the oven to 180°C, Gas Mark 4. Sprinkle your work surface with flour, tip the dough out onto it and roll until it's about 5 millimetres thick. Cut out hearts using a heart-shaped cutter. Gather the trimmings, roll again and cut out more shapes. Place the hearts on the prepared baking sheet and transfer to the oven. After 8–10 minutes gently press down on one of the hearts to test if they're done – if your finger leaves a dent in the biscuit, bake for a little longer.

Transfer the baked hearts to a rack to cool. They will be rock-hard when they come out of the oven, but they will soften a little once cooled and refrigerated. Place the hearts in a container, cover with a damp tea towel, and leave in the fridge for 3–4 days.

When ready to serve, cover in melted dark chocolate, and transfer to a rack. Once the chocolate hardens, the hearts are ready to eat.

#TIP
Only coat the gingerbread hearts you intend to serve immediately. The remaining hearts will keep in the fridge for up to one month.

GINGERBREAD SLICES

These gingerbread slices have been a Christmas favourite at Meyer's Bakeries. People go crazy for their intense honey flavour and lightness. Made from the same dough as the Gingerbread Hearts (see page 253), however, in this recipe the honey, thick layer of chocolate, and spices are accompanied by a coarse apple compote and a soft butter cream. Remember that the pre-dough must be stored for at least one month in order for it to develop the taste and texture that help make the gingerbread slices succulent and soft.

About 20 slices

GINGERBREAD DOUGH
see ingredients on page 253

APPLE COMPOTE
500 g tart cooking apples
250 g sugar
50 g cider vinegar, or to taste

BUTTERCREAM
200 g salted butter, softened
200 g icing sugar

COATING
200 g plain chocolate, preferably 85 per cent
  cocoa solids, melted

APPLE COMPOTE
Peel and core the apples, then roughly chop. Put in a saucepan along with the sugar and cook over a low heat until tender. Mash into a coarse compote and add cider vinegar to taste. Place in a plastic container, seal with a lid and store in the fridge (it should keep for up to 1 month). This is more compote than you'll need for your gingerbread slices, so you can spoon it on to yoghurt, serve it for pudding with a splash of milk or save it for your next batch of gingerbread slices.

BUTTERCREAM
Using an electric hand mixer, cream together the butter and icing sugar until pale and fluffy. (Only make as much as you need, as this cream will quickly go off.)

GINGERBREAD DOUGH
See page 253 for the method.

Grease two baking sheets with a little sunflower oil, dust them with flour and set them aside. Preheat the oven to 180°C, Gas Mark 4. Sprinkle your work surface with flour, tip the dough out onto it and divide it into 4 lumps. Roll these lumps into long thin sticks each approximately 35 cm long. Place two gingerbread sticks on one baking sheet and transfer to the oven. After 12 minutes gently press down on one to test if they're done – if your finger leaves a dent, bake for a little longer. Transfer the baked gingerbread to a rack to cool while you bake the remaining gingerbread sticks. Once all four sticks are baked and have cooled, cover them with a clean damp tea towel and place them in the fridge for 3–4 days.

Take only one gingerbread stick from the fridge at a time. Set it on a baking sheet and split it horizontally down the middle. Lift the top half off and set it aside while you spread the bottom half with apple compote. Then spread the inside of the top half with the butter cream. Sandwich the two halves with their fillings together and cover the whole thing in melted chocolate. Allow the chocolate to harden, cut the stick into five slices and serve.

#TIP
The gingerbread sticks will keep for months in the fridge, so only finish off the slices as you actually need them. And don't return finished slices complete with their chocolate coating to the fridge, as the cold temperature will cause the chocolate to turn grey and attract moisture.

SCONES

The secret to making scones that are cracklingly crisp on the outside and velvety soft, light, and spongy on the inside, is to roll the dough gently by hand. My daughter Elvira taught me this after my own failed attempts had resulted in tough, dense scones. You can add chopped plain chocolate or raisins to the dough or leave it as it is. Serve with butter, clotted cream, and raspberry jam in proper British style.

14 scones

DOUGH
560 g plain flour
85 g caster sugar
25 g baking powder
5 g salt
200 g cold salted butter, from the fridge
375 g cold buttermilk

FILLING (OPTIONAL)
120 g chopped plain chocolate or raisins

BRUSHING
1 egg, beaten

See the following pages on how to knead, shape and bake scones.

HOW TO MAKE SCONES

1. Put the flour, sugar, baking powder and salt into a mixing bowl. Tear the cold butter into small pieces and add to the flour mixture, then leave in the fridge for at least 1 hour, until everything is properly chilled.

2. Add the cold buttermilk, then carefully combine all the ingredients by hand until the dough is cohesive but still rather loose.

3. Sprinkle your work surface with flour and tip the dough out onto it.

4. Carefully roll the dough into a 20 x 50-cm rectangle.

5. Fold one-third of the dough over itself.

6. Fold the other third of the dough over the other layers. Scrape the work surface clean.

7. Sprinkle a little flour on top of the dough and repeat the rolling and folding process three times.

8. If you want to add any fillings to your scones, sprinkle them on top of the dough before doing the folding and rolling process for the last time.

9. Place the folded and rolled dough on a nonstick baking sheet, seam-side down, and leave in the fridge for 15 minutes.

10. Roll the chilled dough until it is approximately 1 cm thick and cut, slice or mould into 14 equally-sized scones.

11. Line a baking sheet with nonstick baking paper and arrange the scones on it, spaced well apart. Brush the top of each scone with some beaten egg.

12. Gently press down the middle of each scone with three fingers to make sure they rise straight up.

13. Bake the scones at 220°C, Gas Mark 7, until golden brown on top, for about 8–10 minutes.

LEFTOVERS

In my family, home-baked bread disappears like snow in sunshine, but on occasions I actually bake too much and then find myself with leftovers. However, avoiding food waste gives me enormous pleasure, so I make sure nothing is ever wasted. For example, I use leftover bread to make rye bread and beer porridge, homemade breadcrumbs, crunchy rye topping and crisp flakes. And rather than putting the starter I don't use after refreshing my stock starter in the bin, I make delicious crisp flakes or tempura. In this way, every last crumb is eaten.

RYE BREAD AND BEER PORRIDGE

Rye bread and beer porridge is a classic Danish dish, and we always ate it for breakfast when I was a child. In later years, this dish has experienced a renaissance in many gourmet restaurants, served as a pudding. This is my updated version, which my parents' generation may not immediately recognize. I've used muscovado sugar and molasses for sweetness, plain chocolate for a hint of bitterness and finished it all off with cream.

8 small portions

INGREDIENTS
500 g rye bread
500 g light beer
150 g muscovado sugar or dark brown sugar
50 g molasses
100 g double cream, warmed
cider vinegar, to taste
salt, optional

SERVE IT WITH
whipped cream
grated plain chocolate, preferably 85 per cent
   cocoa solids

Tear the rye bread into pieces and add to a bowl. Pour in enough beer to cover the bread, and leave to soak overnight.

Place the soaked rye bread in a wire sieve set over a large bowl and leave to drain (reserve the beer for later). Add the rye bread to a blender, along with the sugar, molasses and cream. Blend until completely smooth. If the mass is too thick and difficult to blend, add a little of the reserved beer. The texture should resemble thick pancake batter. Pour the porridge into a saucepan over a low heat and carefully warm it up. Add cider vinegar to taste and a little salt, if you like.

Top the rye bread and beer porridge with whipped cream or a scoop of vanilla ice cream and sprinkle with grated chocolate to serve.

BREADCRUMBS

Being transformed into homemade breadcrumbs
is a fine destiny for any high-quality bread.
It's so easy to make and so much better than
the chemically treated, preservative-laden
breadcrumbs you buy at the supermarket. All you
have to do is dry the bread in the oven and then
crumble it in a blender or a mincer, and you have
breadcrumbs you can use as a coating for pan-fried
fish. You can even make sugar-coated breadcrumbs
to sprinkle on puddings.

INGREDIENTS
leftover dry white bread

Remove the crusts and tear the bread into small pieces. Line a baking sheet
with nonstick baking paper and spread the pieces of bread all across it.
Bake in a very low oven for 3–4 hours, or until completely dry. Once the bread
has cooled, add it to a blender and blend it into crumbs.

These breadcrumbs will keep at least 4–6 weeks sealed in an
airtight container.

CRUNCHY RYE TOPPING

Do not despair if the end of your loaf of rye bread has become a little dry. Think of it as a unique opportunity to create a highly versatile crunchy topping with lovely sour, sweet, bitter, and salty flavours.

Makes about 300 g

INGREDIENTS
250 g rye bread
50 g dark cane sugar or dark brown sugar
30 g molasses
3 g salt

Chop the rye bread or blend it in a blender until it turns into coarse breadcrumbs, then mix in the sugar, molasses and salt. Line a baking sheet with nonstick baking paper, spread the crumbs evenly across it, and bake in a very low oven for 3–4 hours, or until completely dry.

Remove from the oven and leave to cool before sprinkling it on top of ice cream, yoghurt or any dairy product of your choice.

This crunchy topping will keep for 4–6 weeks sealed in an airtight container.

BREAD CRISPS

Very thin, crisp, butter-roasted slices of day-old bread make a wonderful side to go with soup or salad. You could even enjoy them as a snack or for scooping up all types of sauces and dips.

INGREDIENTS
day-old bread of any kind
a little melted salted butter
salt

Slice the bread very thinly with a sharp breadknife or use a mandolin slicer. Spread the bread slices out on a baking sheet lined with nonstick parchment paper. Brush them with melted butter and sprinkle with salt. Bake the slices in the oven at 130°C, Gas Mark ½, for about 30 minutes, or until golden and crisp.

#TIP
Browning the butter before brushing it onto the bread slices adds another flavour dimension. You could even add a little crushed garlic or some of your favourite spices to the butter.

WHEAT CRISPS

Don't bin that surplus starter after refreshing
it! Instead, use it to make these very thin, crisp
leavened crisps. You can serve them with almost
anything, such as soups and salads, and you can
dip them in lovely sauces as a pre-dinner snack.
They also keep hungry children quiet until their
dinner is ready.

1 sheet

INGREDIENTS
200 g wheat starter
a little plain flour
salt

Pour the starter into a mixing bowl and beat lightly while adding a little flour.
The amount of flour you need to add depends on how thick your starter is.
Continue adding flour until the texture is like thick pancake batter. Finally add
a little salt to taste.

Pour the finished batter into a large baking tray lined with nonstick baking
paper and use a spatula to smooth it down and push it into all the corners.
Place the tray on the middle shelf of the oven and bake at 140°C, Gas Mark 1,
for about 25 minutes, or until golden. Leave to cool before breaking into
smaller crisps.

#TIP
If the hot air is making the paper rise while the wheat crisps are in the oven, put
something heavy along the edges to keep it down while baking. Just be sure whatever
you use to do this is ovenproof.

VEGETABLE TEMPURA

You can reduce food waste by using your surplus starter to make these wonderfully crisp and delicate vegetable snacks. Just about any vegetable you like will work, so this recipe also gives you a chance to clear out the crisper drawer in your fridge. This tempura makes a great appetizer, goes down well with a beer or drinks before dinner and makes a quick and easy afternoon snack for the kids.

INGREDIENTS
200 g starter
plain flour
salt
neutral oil, for deep frying
a mixture of vegetables, cut into smaller pieces

Start by checking the texture of the starter. It should be like thick pancake batter. If it's too thin, you can add a little extra plain flour to thicken it. Add salt to taste.

Pour about 1.5 cm of oil into a deep saucepan and heat until it's about 150°C. Dip the vegetables in the starter. Using a long-handled slotted spoon, add them a few pieces at a time directly to the hot oil. Fry until golden on both sides then remove them from the pan and place on a plate lined with kitchen paper while you fry the remaining pieces. Serve the fried vegetables immediately, while crisp and fresh.

#TIP
If you're not sure whether or not to add salt to your starter, start by frying a little on its own. Taste it for saltiness and if it needs more, stir some in before dipping the vegetables in it.

USEFUL INFORMATION

On the following pages we have put together information that is not strictly necessary in order to achieve a good result when you are baking. However, it is knowledge that can give you a better understanding of what happens when you mix, rise, prove and shape your dough, and bake your bread or buns. Here you can read about everything from autolyse and wild yeast, gluten networks and falling numbers to the best way to store your bread.

USEFUL INFORMATION

AUTOLYSE

Autolyse is a mixing method, where you let the dough rest before mixing it. Use this method if you really want to pamper your dough and reduce the time you spend pummelling it with a wooden spoon or have the mixer running.

Autolyse works particularly well with the wheat doughs in the chapters on wheat bread and whole-grain bread. For example, we use it in the method for By Hand – The Gentle Method (see page 58). You should not use autolyse for rye bread doughs, however, because in this case it is not the gluten strands that makes the dough rise, so the dough does not benefit from resting.

While the dough is resting, the starch in the flour and the gluten strands gradually absorb a large part of the moisture in the dough in preparation to be mixed. This means the dough starts to create the gluten network by itself, without you touching it.

Note that you do not add salt to the dough until after resting. The salt tightens up the gluten network, and if you wait before adding it, the gluten strands remain soft so they are better able to absorb moisture during the resting period. Once the flour has absorbed the moisture and the gluten network has begun to form, we want it to be as tight and strong as possible.

How to proceed

Put flour, water, yeast and starter into a mixing bowl and mix together quickly to a smooth dough with no lumps of flour. Cover the mixing bowl loosely with a tea towel or a lid and leave at room temperature for 30 minutes to 1 hour.

Now add the salt and mix the dough, using one of the methods described on pages 55–58. Regardless of which mixing method you choose, using autolyse means you only have to mix the dough for a shorter time in order to obtain a strong gluten network than if you mix all the ingredients together at the start and begin mixing immediately.

FINE OR COARSE SALT

If you use fine salt, just add it to the dough after the resting period, but if you use coarse salt, you should reserve 50 g of the water when mixing the ingredients at the start. Dissolve the salt in the water and add the solution to the dough after the resting period, before you begin to mix.

FALLING NUMBER

The falling number is a measurement taken by the grain miller, and indicates how many seconds it takes for a piece of specialist equipment to fall through a cooked paste made from the flour being tested and water. The number shows whether the grain had begun to sprout before milling, which reduces the baking quality of the flour.

Moisture and sprouting

When cereal plants are growing in the field, the individual grains drop down into the damp soil, germinate and grow up into a new plant in order to ensure the survival of the plant species. The fact that the farmer comes along and harvests the kernels so that we can grind it into flour and make bread from it is not something the plant had intended.

If the summer is wet, or if it rains during the grain harvest so it gets damp, the grain mistakenly believes that it has already fallen into the soil. It prepares to sprout by producing a lot of enzymes designed to speed up the conversion of the starch in the grain into the sugars that provide nourishment for the sprouting seeds. If too many of these enzymes are produced before the grain is ground into flour, problems arise when making the flour into bread. This happens because there is a short phase during baking when the starch is converted to sugars, and if there are too many enzymes in the flour this process becomes slightly too efficient and too much starch is converted into sugars. This means that there is not enough starch left in the dough to absorb all the moisture, because sugars cannot absorb moisture in the same way as starch. As a result, the bread becomes pasty, even if it has been baked long enough, In addition, the sugars give it a taste that is slightly too sweet.
The falling number is particularly relevant to rye flour. Rye grains are much more inclined to

sprout than, say, wheat grains, so there is a much greater risk that the quality of rye flour will be adversely affected by unfavourable weather conditions during ripening and harvest.

Falling-number analysis

After harvest, the miller will often undertake a falling-number analysis of the grain to see whether it has begun to sprout and is therefore 'harvest-damaged', as it is known. The analysis is carried out by simulating baking and making a paste of the flour. If there is high enzyme activity in the flour, a lot of the starch will have been converted to sugars. In that case, there will be less starch remaining to thicken the paste, and it will be relatively thin. If there is less enzyme activity, a smaller amount of the starch will have been converted, so the paste will thicken and become more viscous.

The actual analysis takes place in a falling-number apparatus. This is a tube, which is filled with the paste made from the flour to be tested. A plunger is sunk down through the paste at a specific pressure. The thicker the paste, the longer it takes for the plunger to reach the bottom. The number of seconds it takes is called the falling number. So a high number indicates a thick 'slow' paste, due to low enzyme activity, and is therefore a sign of good-quality flour.

Good and bad harvest years

The falling number can vary widely from season to season, depending on how wet the summer has been and whether it was also very wet when the grain was harvested. The big flour mills and production plants have plenty of storage space, so they can store grain from both the good years and the bad years and mix them together, so their flour is of uniform quality with a sufficiently high falling number every year. The smaller flour producers rarely have enough storage space to store grain from year to year, so the quality of their flour may vary. However, flour with a falling number that is poor enough to cause major problems does not normally find its way on to the market.

Starter and salt

Unfortunately, we consumers cannot see on a bag of flour whether it contains flour with a high or low falling number. So, if you have baked a successful rye bread and make it again using exactly the same recipe, there is a chance that the next time you will end up with a soggy crumb, because this time the flour had a lower falling number. However, if this happens, there are two ingredients that you add

HOW TO REMEDY A LOW FALLING NUMBER

Let the starter stand for up to 5–6 hours longer before adding it to the dough. This allows it to become more acidic.

• Substitute 20–25 per cent of the rye flour with whole-grain wheat flour, which typically has a much higher falling time than rye flour, so it takes longer for the starch to be converted to sugars during baking, thus reducing the risk of a soggy crumb.

• Add a little extra rye flour to the dough to yield a firmer dough – but be aware that this also makes rye bread drier.

to your rye bread dough anyway, which you can use to prevent the starch breaking down too quickly during baking. These are a starter, which contributes acid, and salt. Both acid and salt inhibit enzyme activity and if you increase the amount of both you can counteract the effect of a low falling number.

#CHECK THE INTERNAL TEMPERATURE
We recommend using a baking thermometer when you bake rye bread. When the internal temperature reaches 97–98°C, you can be sure that your rye bread is done. However, if the loaf is still soggy, it is probably due to the fact that you have been unfortunate enough to get hold of some rye flour with too low a falling number. Therefore, you can exclude the possibility that it is because you did not bake your rye bread for long enough.

PHYTIN AND PHYTASE
One of the great advantages of allowing the dough to rise for a long time when making bread is that your loaf not only tastes better and has more flavour, it is also healthier. Flour, and especially the coarse pieces of the husk of the grain, contain something called phytic acid, which retains or 'locks' some of the minerals (calcium, zinc and iron) in the flour and the grains so the body cannot absorb them. However, if you let the dough rise for at least 10 hours or pre-soak whole grains for at least 10 hours, the phytic acid is broken down by the enzyme phytase, which is found naturally in flour and cereals.

So, if you bake two loaves with exactly the same ingredients and let one rise for a short time while letting the other rise for 10 hours, the loaf with the longer rising time will be healthier to eat.

GLUTEN AND GLUTEN NETWORK
One of the things most people love about bread is a light, porous crumb full of aromatic air holes. This is a way of using grain that is somewhat different from – and more delicious than – the wet porridge that people in prehistoric times baked on hot stones to make a kind of flatbread. So it was a great step forward when the Ancient Egyptians discovered how to make a dough that could rise and yield an airy bread.

Two things are needed in order to produce airy bread: some yeast cells to produce carbon dioxide, and something to retain the carbon dioxide in the dough, so it does not just seep out but remains in the dough and causes it to rise.

Wheat is the best species of cereal for making airy bread. This is because when water is added to wheat flour the dough produces gluten, and when the dough is mixed, the gluten strands arrange themselves into a network of rubbery, elastic membranes – rather like bubbles of chewing gum – that capture the carbon dioxide and form pockets of air inside the loaf. When the bread is baked, the gluten network sets, retaining the air holes.

What is gluten?
Wheat flour does not contain gluten as such. However, there are two proteins in wheat flour, glutenin and gliadin. When water is added to the flour, they swell up and become gluten. The two proteins work together but each has its own function in the dough. Glutenin makes the dough elastic, pulling it together so it keeps its shape and does not spread. Gliadin makes it possible for the dough to be stretched without falling apart and to be formed into a loaf.

To get an idea of how the gluten network works, imagine the gluten strands as elastic bands that have been cut into small pieces. When the ingredients for the dough have just been mixed together, the pieces are lying in a big untidy heap. When the dough is mixed and stretched, the gluten strands gradually arrange themselves into a system in which they stick together – both head to tail to form long strings, and side-on with other neighbouring strands lying in the same direction – resulting in a cohesive 'mat' of gluten. These gluten mats form in layers – rather like plywood – and it is between these layers that the air bubbles are caught in the dough. The more systematically and tidily the gluten strands are arranged, the stronger the gluten network, the better the dough retains the carbon dioxide, and the airier the resulting bread.

When you have mixed the dough and you think it is ready, you can do a gluten test to check whether you really have mixed the dough enough. This is particularly good if you have mixed the dough in a food stand mixer – it is a bit harder to do the gluten test if you mix the dough gently by hand, because in this case the dough will already have begun to rise a little while you are mixing.

Gluten test
To do the gluten test, dip your hands in a little water and pull the dough out very slowly, carefully, and gently, rather like a piece of chewing gum, until it becomes as transparent as parchment paper and you can see a very thin, cohesive gluten network. If you manage to stretch the dough like this, it is perfectly mixed and ready for rising.

The gluten network strengthens with time
It is not only when you mix and pull the dough that the gluten strands organize themselves systematically and form a network. Time is also a beneficial factor, as the gluten strands will slowly arrange themselves more and more systematically and form the gluten network if the dough just stands for long enough, even without being mixed or pulled. This is the method used for so-called 'no-knead bread'. You will not get a very strong gluten network in this way, but it will be robust enough for you to be able to bake a reasonably airy loaf, especially if you bake it in a loaf tin or cast iron casserole with a lid. However, it is not a method we use at Meyer's Bakeries, as we like to have a stronger gluten network and airier bread.

Over-mixed gluten network
Even though it is important to mix the dough thoroughly in order to get a good, strong gluten network, you should mix it methodically and with care – there is a limit to how much mixing the gluten network/dough can take. If the dough is mixed too much, the gluten strands will be torn apart at the point where they join head to tail. As a result, the dough will lose its elasticity and become a thin, floppy, disconnected mush that cannot be stretched out. When you do the gluten test, you will not see the fine gluten network and the dough will immediately split in two when you try to stretch it.

It is only when using a mixer that you may accidentally over-mix the dough (you would have to mix for a long time by hand before this could happen). However, with a mixer it only takes a few seconds from when the dough looks fine until it becomes overworked. That is why we recommend that you watch for the dough to start to come away from the inside of the mixing bowl and collect round the hook. At that point, stop mixing.

After mixing, when the dough is rising in the refrigerator, the gluten network will quietly carry on strengthening, so there is no reason to risk over-mixing the dough in the mixer – it is always better to stop the mixer sooner rather than later. This also means you can save your energy if you are mixing by hand and let the rising do the rest of the hard work.

OVER-MIXED DOUGH CANNOT BE RESCUED
Unfortunately, if you have over-mixed your dough, you cannot rescue it. Adding more flour to the dough that now feels thin will not help, nor will baking it in a loaf tin. The result will not be good and it would be a waste of time, good flour, and electricity to try.

Types of wheat flour and protein
There are big variations in the quantity and quality of protein in flours, so it makes a difference which flour you use. There must be enough protein in the flour and

the quality must be sufficiently good if the dough is to be strong and elastic.

The quantity of protein in wheat flour depends on which species or wheat variety the flour is made from. There are also two additional factors that help to produce a high protein content: the grain must have had many hours of sunshine, and sufficient nitrogen. Growing in long hours of sunshine gives Italian and French wheat flour a higher protein content than Danish wheat flour which grows in a cooler climate.

The quality of the protein, and consequently the gluten, in the flour depends on the wheat variety. Quality is inherited, so to speak, and even a lot of sunshine and fertilizer will never be able to elevate a variety with poor baking quality to a good baking flour.

For bread, we prefer to use wheat flour with a protein content of 12 per cent. This matches up very well with the wheat we harvest in Scandinavia, which is grown with a view to being as good as possible for baking. In the past there was a tendency for both professional and home bakers to want wheat flour with the highest possible protein content for bread-making. However, many people have gradually come to realize that if they keep to the slightly lower protein content that we use, it is easier to get the lovely big holes in the bread that we love so much, a moister crumb and a bread that is easier for people with a sensitivity to gluten to digest.

#TIP

Check the protein content on the label when you buy wheat flour. For bread, the flour needs a protein content of 12 per cent to withstand being mixed for a long time in order to produce the tough doughs that result in moist, airy bread.

Rye flour

Rye flour behaves in a slightly different way from wheat flour when you mix it and bake with it. The proteins found in rye flour are not of the same type, so in this case it is not possible to obtain a strong gluten network to make the bread airy. Fortunately rye flour contains another substance to make up for it, pentosans (see page 287), which are able to retain some of the carbon dioxide.

YEAST

Yeast is something else we cannot do without when baking bread—without yeast we cannot make bread with the porous crumb and large air holes that we love.

We use two different kinds of yeast in our bread. One is baking yeast that you buy in shops and is usually available in an ordinary and an organic version, and the other is natural yeast or wild yeast, which is found in starters. Both of them are yeasts, so it is not accurate for people say, "I don't bake with yeast, I bake with a starter", because there is yeast in a starter too, just a different kind.

Both kinds of yeast have the same function in our doughs: they feed on the sugar in the flour and produce carbon dioxide, which makes the dough rise, and they give the loaves more taste by creating alcohol in the dough, which adds special flavourings.

Baking yeast

Baking yeast consists of cultivated yeast fungi. There are enormous numbers of these – several million – in every package or sachet. It is potent and easy to use. As previously mentioned, baking yeast is available in both ordinary and organic versions and the differences between them concern both the taste they give to the bread and the impact of their production on the environment.

As a rule, ordinary baking yeast is a monoculture that only contains one kind of yeast cells and this can give the finished bread a rather bland taste. Organic yeast is usually made from wheat and contains several different strains of yeast. This results in a more complex and subtle flavour, which is almost fruity, in some cases. Unlike ordinary yeast, the production of organic yeast does not produce a lot of nitrogen, which is damaging to the environment. Because of both the stronger flavour and the lower environmental impact, we prefer to use organic baking yeast in Meyer's Bakeries.

#TIP

You should use the same quantity of yeast, whether you choose ordinary or organic.

WHAT HAPPENS TO YEAST AT DIFFERENT TEMPERATURES

• At 4°C the yeast process is almost at a standstill. That is why we let the dough rise in the fridge at around 5°C, so the yeast process evolves very slowly. This allows the lactic acid bacteria from the flour and the starter to develop the flavour in the dough gradually.

• The yeast develops at the fastest rate between 20–40°C, so we leave the dough to stand at room temperature on the work surface if we want it to rise quickly or if it needs to be speeded up a little before baking and after proofing in the fridge.

• When the bread first goes into the hot oven, the heat gives the yeast cells a kick, so they produce a little more carbon dioxide and make the bread rise the last little bit. When the temperature of the loaf has reached 60°C, the yeast cells die, but by then the proteins in the gluten network have set so the loaf does not collapse.

• When the temperature of the loaf has reached 80°C, all the alcohol will have evaporated, but it will have left behind a delicious aroma that helps give the bread a good flavour.

Wild yeast cells from a starter

If you want to bake bread using a starter, it must contain a sufficient quantity of wild yeast cells. In the starter chapter on pages 42–3 you can read all about wild yeast and how to refresh your starter in order to increase the number of wild yeast cells until it contains enough of them for you to be able to bake with it.

What does the yeast do in your dough?

With both baking yeast and wild yeast, as long as there is oxygen in the dough, the yeast 'eats' sugar (from the starch in the flour) and oxygen and converts or breaks it down into water, carbon dioxide and alcohol. After a short time, when there is no oxygen left, the yeast continues to live on the sugar, which is now broken down into carbon dioxide and alcohol.

The carbon dioxide is captured during both processes, either in the gluten network (see page 280) in the dough for wheat loaves, so the crumb becomes airy and porous, or by the pentosans in the elastic dough for rye loaves so they rise.

The alcohol, which is in the form of a gas, is captured along with the carbon dioxide in the small air pockets in the crumb, and therefore plays a considerable part in adding flavour to the bread.

#TIP

If you want to experiment when you bake, try reducing the amount of yeast from time to time to see how little yeast you actually need in your dough. The amount of yeast required is dependent on a number of factors, such as the kind of yeast you are using, the ingredients in the recipe and the interaction between them, as well as how warm the surrounding air temperature is when the dough is rising.

THE HYDRATION OF A DOUGH

Hydration	WHAT THE DOUGH AND BREAD IS LIKE
60 %	This yields a classic dough. Gives a heavy, substantial dough that you can shape and prove in a baking tin. Children enjoy working with it as they can roll and shape the dough. The bread will have a very uniform crumb without large holes.
70 %	You can still shape and stretch the dough and it can prove unsupported on a baking tin. The bread will have slightly larger holes and a moister crumb.
80 %	It will be more difficult to shape the dough and let it prove unsupported. If the dough is thoroughly mixed, the bread will have a fine, almost transparent crumb and a lovely crust that stays nice and crisp once baked.
90 %	The dough will be too wet and loose to prove in a baking tin. The dough needs to have risen well in a bowl and be handled carefully, so as not to squeeze the air out of it when you cut it in pieces and shape the loaf. This will give your bread a very fine, moist crumb but the crust will go soft quickly.
100 %	The dough should be handled as for 90 per cent, but in this case it really takes practice not to squeeze too much air out of it. The loaf will need to be baked in a very hot oven. If you are successful, you will be rewarded with a fantastic flavour, a lovely moist crumb and bread that stays fresh for a long time.

HYDRATION

The hydration of a dough is a figure that provides some information about its softness or firmness. The figure indicates how much liquid – usually water – there is in the dough in proportion to the amount of flour, with both indicated by weight. Hydration is shown as a percentage, so in a dough with 1 kg flour and 850 g water, the hydration will be 85 per cent and in a dough with 600 g flour and 600 g water, it will be 100 per cent. So if there is more water than flour in a recipe, it means that the hydration is over 100 per cent.

On the basis of these calculations, with the help of a calculator or mental arithmetic, you can quickly decode any recipe (not just the ones in this book) and get an idea of what kind of dough is involved – whether it is a moist dough or a recipe for a firmer dough. Whole-grain flour can absorb a lot more water than regular flour, so the amount of whole-grain flour in the recipe matters, as it will slightly change the consistency of the dough. However, the difference is not that large and the hydration figure is still a good indicator of how wet the dough is; the figure can be used to compare the doughs in various recipes, even when slightly different proportions of whole-grain flour are used.

Advantages and disadvantages of high and low hydration – wet and drier doughs

At Meyer's Bakeries we typically bake our wheat and whole-grain bread using a very wet dough with a hydration of 90 per cent or more. The advantages of having a lot of liquid in the dough are that it gives the bread a moister crumb with a lovely consistency and large air holes, and at the same time, the aromas in the flour develop better in the wet dough, giving the bread a richer flavour. The finished bread also keeps longer than bread with less liquid in the dough.

The disadvantages of having a lot of liquid in the dough are that wet doughs are slightly more difficult to handle than firmer doughs, until you have had a certain amount of practice. In addition, the crust of the baked bread will become soft more quickly, because some of the moisture from the crumb will seep into the crust and makes it damp. However, you can compensate for this by quickly warming the whole loaf in the oven or serving the bread toasted, so the crust becomes crisp again.

Experimenting with the amount of water

You can certainly be flexible with the amounts of water we use in the wet doughs in the recipes for wheat and whole-grain bread and still end up with really nice bread. If you do not have very much experience with wet dough, it is a really good idea to start by adding a little less water to the dough than the recipe calls for, so you get a slightly firmer dough. It is easier to shape than wet dough, which can be a bit difficult to get into the oven without squeezing the air out of it. Then, when you have been successful a few times with a little less water, you can add a little more water, and in that way move gradually towards a wetter dough. If you are brave enough, you can even try using more water than it calls for in the recipes. In our baking courses we get really good results when making wet doughs with a hydration right up to 100 per cent, i.e. 500 g water to 500 g flour.

#TIP

If you are weighing your ingredients on digital kitchen scales, you may as well weigh the water too. This is a more precise way of measuring water compared with using a measuring cup.

MALT POWDER

Malt powder (which is like a flour) is most commonly made from barley grains but it can also be made from other types of cereal. To make malt powder, the grains are moistened so they begin to sprout, which means that most of the starch in the grains converts into sugars. After some time, the sprouted grains are dried and heat-treated by roasting them. The length of time they are roasted depends on what the malt is to be used for. During roasting the sugar in the grains caramelizes, giving the malt powder its characteristic aroma. Finally, the malt grains are ground into malt powder or made into malt syrup. Both products are now available in most supermarkets and health-food shops.

MALT FLOUR OR MALT SYRUP

As a rule of thumb you should use five times as much malt syrup as malt flour, i.e. 5 g malt flour to every 25 g malt syrup.

Malt flour may be dark or light and there are great differences between the two types, so it is important to use them correctly. For example, if you use the light type in your rye bread, there is a risk that it will produce a damp, sticky crumb.

The type of malt we use in our rye bread is dark, burnt malt, which gives the rye bread flavour, character and colour. It is also known as enzyme inactive malt, because the grains are roasted and burnt hard so that the sugar caramelizes and the only function of the malt in the bread is to give it flavour and a darker colour. In the UK you can buy dark malt flour from Wessex Mill, see page 291.

The other type of malt, which is also known as an enzyme-active malt, is lighter and does not receive such a harsh heat treatment. When used in dough, it stimulates the breakdown of starch into sugars during baking (see page 278), and that is definitely not something we want when baking with rye. Therefore, use it sparingly when making rye bread. Light malt is typically used in more classic, firmer doughs, which have a lot of flour and not as much water – the malt helps to break down the starch, giving the loaves a moister crumb. Light, enzyme-active malt can also be used to kick-start the yeast process (see page 283).

The doughs we work with at Meyer's Bakeries contain so much water that the loaves become moist all by themselves, and since we are not interested in making the loaves rise quickly, we do not use enzyme-active malt in our recipes.

WHAT HAPPENS TO BREAD AFTER BAKING?

As soon as you take your loaf out of the oven, various processes start happening in the bread, which gradually make it feel drier and consequently less interesting to eat. Here we tell you a little about these processes and how to store your bread in order to retain as much moisture as possible in freshly baked bread.

There are two reasons why bread will dry out after baking. Firstly, some of the water in the bread slowly evaporates and disappears. Secondly, when bread is baked, the starch in the bread crystallizes – a process known as retrogradation.

Retrogradation

The moment the bread comes out of the oven its structure begins to change. All the water absorbed by the starch in the flour during baking slowly migrates out of the starch grains again, so they crystallize and 'retrograde' back into something resembling the state they were in before they absorbed the water. As the starch grains continue to dry out, the bread will not only feel drier, but will become drier as you chew it, the longer it has been left standing. The water that migrates out of the starch grains is still in the bread but in a state where it no longer helps make the bread feel moist.

Storage temperatures

The speed at which the bread retrogrades and starts to feel dry when you chew it depends very much on the temperature at which it is stored. This process happens most quickly at 4–7°C, so keeping bread in the fridge is the worst place to store your bread if you want to keep it moist.

Room temperature is the best temperature to store bread. Here retrogradation happens more slowly than in the fridge, so the bread stays moist longer.

If you keep bread in a paper bag or rolled up in a cloth, the crust will stay crisp for longer than if you put it in a plastic bag. With plastic, the water evaporating from the bread will produce condensation inside the bag, so the crust will become soft more quickly.

If you are not expecting to eat the whole loaf for one or two days, you can put the part of the bread you want to keep a bit longer in a plastic bag and put it in the fridge. But, hang on a minute – can that be right? Yes, because although the bread certainly dries out more quickly in the fridge than if it is standing on the work surface at room temperature, it will also have a longer 'shelf life', so it will take longer before the bread starts to grow mould. This means you must discriminate between how long it takes the bread to dry out and how it keeps longest.

The freezer is a good place to store bread if you want to keep it for more than 4 to 5 days. There are two things that are important when freezing bread. Firstly, make sure the bread cools down to below 0°C as quickly as possible. In this way you avoid the bread remaining too long in the zone around 4–7°C, where crystallization is particularly rapid. Secondly, you must bear the same point in mind when thawing the frozen bread – get it up to room temperature as quickly as possible, so you pass rapidly through the 4–7°C zone.

Reheating

If the bread has been standing on the work surface for more than two days, the crumb will probably have become drier as a result of retrogradation. However, if you warm up the bread so the crumb reaches a temperature of above 60°C, the starch grains will swell up again and absorb some of the water that is still in the bread (but only in a state where it does not help to make it moist). This is what happens when you heat a slice of dry bread in a toaster and the dry bread is magically given new life and the inside regains its soft, moist consistency.

When re-heating bread, use the same method, whether it has been standing for 2 to 3 days at room temperature or 4 to 5 days in the fridge. Put the bread into a preheated oven at 200°C, Gas Mark 6, and it will become delicious once again. If you like, you can rub the crust with a little water before putting the bread in the oven.

If your bread has been in the freezer, you should ensure that it is completely thawed before you heat it up, otherwise the procedure is exactly the same: into a hot oven at 200°C, Gas Mark 6, until the bread is thoroughly warmed through and the heat reaches right into the middle.

#ONLY ONE CHANCE

Note that you can only warm the bread up once for a good result – there is not enough moisture in the bread to do this more than once. If you only intend to eat part of the loaf, do not warm up the whole thing.

PENTOSANS

Rye flour does not have the same strong types of gluten and therefore the same baking properties as wheat flour. So when you make doughs with a high proportion of rye flour, it is not possible to obtain a strong gluten network (see page 282) of the kind you have in a wheat dough, which can retain the carbon dioxide from the yeast and produce an airy bread. On the other hand, rye flour contains a large number of pentosans, which we can use to make the bread rise.

Pentosans are a kind of water-soluble dietary fibre, which can absorb a good deal of water, and they are part of the reason why rye dough sticks to your fingers and is difficult to wash off your hands. It is the same gluey effect that inhibits the gluten in the rye and stops it forming a good gluten network. However, at the same time the pentosans contribute positively to the rye dough in several ways. The first is that, as previously mentioned, they absorb a lot of liquid, and this means the rye bread becomes moist and can keep fresh and good to eat for a long time. The second very important thing is that the water-soluble carbohydrates in the pentosans give the rye dough a slightly elastic consistency, which allows the dough to capture the carbon dioxide from the yeast and make the bread nice and airy. While this cannot be compared with the airiness that wheat bread gets from the gluten network in the wheat, it is sufficient to make the crumb of the rye bread porous and not heavy and sticky.

In addition to helping with the structure of rye bread, the pentosans supply you with a nutritionally valuable dietary fibre, which helps keep your blood sugar levels stable.

SALT

Salt is not the world's healthiest ingredient so it is not something you should add to your food without thinking. However, if used in the right quantities, salt helps to bring out and enhance the flavour of cereals and produce a delicious bread with much more character. Salt is also important for obtaining a good crumb. This applies to both wheat bread and rye bread but in different ways.

Salt in wheat bread

When the dough rises, there are a number of enzymes that split the starch in the flour into sugars, which the yeast lives on. Salt reduces the speed at which the yeast 'eats' the sugars (and this applies to both baking yeast and the yeast in a starter). So, by adding salt to the dough, we avoid it rising too fast and we have a lovely long rising time where the aromas in the dough are allowed to develop giving the bread maximum flavour. Since yeast does not manage to eat all the sugar, there will be more of it left in the dough, which gives the bread a darker crust in a good way, as well as a better taste. The aromas from the crust also penetrate the crumb and in this way the salt helps to make the whole loaf really flavoursome.

Salt also strengthens the gluten network. This is an advantage when baking with some of the heritage varieties, which have a slightly soft gluten structure. When the salt helps to make the gluten network stronger, it means that the bread will be airier and have a firmer crumb.

Salt in rye bread

It is especially important to have enough salt in rye bread dough (see page 278). If the rye flour has too low a falling number, there will come a point during baking when too high a proportion of the starch splits into sugars, and the rye bread will taste too sweet and go sticky, however long you bake it for. Salt and acid limit the amount of starch that is split into sugars, so it is very important for the structure of rye bread to have enough salt in the dough.

#TIP

If you feel that some of the recipes in the book taste a little too salty, simply adjust the recipes to suit your taste. However, when it comes to rye bread, it is a good idea to add a little more starter, if you cut down on the amount of salt.

WHEN IS THE BREAD READY?

It can be hard to judge when a loaf is completely baked. Baking times depend on the shape of the loaf and they also vary from one oven to another. Our recommendation is that if in doubt, it is better to slightly over-bake the bread than under-bake. With the wet types of dough we use in this book, you have no need to fear that the bread will become too dry.

It is normal to let the crust become really dark in colour when baking. It gives the bread a distinctive taste and also ensures that the bread has finished baking.

WHAT HAPPENS IN WHEAT BREAD WHEN YOU BAKE IT?

30–40°C	The temperature of the dough rises slowly and the yeast cells are very active.
50–60°C	The yeast cells work more and more slowly, and die out.
55° C	The gluten network stiffens into the 'skeleton' of the loaf and begins to lose the liquid that is to be absorbed by the starch.
50–70° C	The starch begins to gelatinize (absorb) the liquid in the bread and at the same time there is activity in the enzymes that break down some of the starch into sugars.
80°C	The alcohol produced during the breakdown of the starch evaporates, leaving a delicate aroma in the bread.
80–90°C	The enzyme activity and the breakdown of starch into sugar stops.
90°C	The starch stops gelatinizing (absorbing liquid).
100°C	The water in the dough begins to evaporate.

When you pick up the loaf, it should feel airy and "light" (it is rather hard to describe in words) and when you tap the crust it should sound hollow.

Use a thermometer
A good way of judging how long the bread needs to bake before it is ready is to measure the core temperature of the bread using a kitchen thermometer. Stick the tip of the thermometer into the exact centre of the loaf—this spot is the last to finish baking. This way you can be sure that the entire loaf is ready when the core reaches the right temperature. When you have used the thermometer and practiced on a few loaves to get to know how the bread should feel when it is ready, you will be able to assess it just by lifting the loaf without the aid of the thermometer. However, when you bake rye bread, it can be a bit difficult to assess when the bread is perfectly baked using only your senses. Here it is a good idea to use a thermometer and take the bread out as soon as the temperature has reached 97°C.

Use your senses – and set the timer
If you want to have a perfectly baked loaf, it is not a good idea to set the timer to the recommended baking time and then take the bread out when the timer ends. Instead, use your senses to check whether the loaf is ready. Use your eyes to judge the colour of the crust, your nose to assess the aroma and your hands to check whether the loaf feels as light as it should. Instead, set the timer to end at the point when you are about to start using your senses to check if the bread is ready.

CORE TEMPERATURES IN FINISHED BREAD
In order to be certain that your bread is ready, the various types of bread should reach the following temperatures:

Wheat bread	99–100°C
Whole-grain bread	100°C
Rye bread	97–98°C

USEFUL ADDRESSES

MEYER'S BAKING SCHOOLS

Meyers Madhus
Nørrebrogade 52
2200 Copenhagen N
www.meyersmadhus.dk

Meyers Bageri Commissary
38-40 10th Street
Long Island City, NY 11101
United States
www.greatnorthernfood.com

MEYER'S BAKERIES & DELIS

Meyers Bageri
Amagerbrogade 48
2300 Copenhagen S

Meyers Bageri
Classensgade 33
2100 Copenhagen Ø

Meyers Bageri
Gl. Kongevej 103
1850 Frederiksberg

Meyers Bageri
Jægersborggade 9
2200 Copenhagen N

Meyers Bageri
St. Kongensgade 46
1264 Copenhagen K

Meyers Deli
Gl. Kongevej 107
1850 Frederiksberg

Meyers i Lyngby
Lyngby Hovedgade 49
2800 Kgs. Lyngby

Meyers Bageri at Great Northern Food Hall
Grand Central Terminal
Vanderbilt Hall
89 East 42nd Street,
New York, NY 10017

Meyers Bageri
667 Driggs Avenue,
Brooklyn, NY 11211

BAKING EQUIPMENT SUPPLIERS

Bread Matters
Macbiehill Farmhouse
Lamancha, West Linton
Peebleshire EH46 7AZ
+44 (0)1968 660449
www.breadmatters.com
As well as offering courses and running campaigns (see page 292), Bread Matters operates an online shop selling proving baskets, tins, baking stones, grain mills, peels and brushes, scrapers and blades, as well as sourdough starter.

Lakeland
Alexandra Buildings
Windermere, Cumbria, LA23 1BQ
+44 (0)15394 88100
www.lakeland.co.uk
National retailer of bread-baking tools and equipment with stores throughout the UK. Products can also be ordered online

FLOUR AND GRAIN SUPPLIERS

Bacheldre Watermill
Churchstoke,
Mongomery, Powys, SY15 5TE
+44 (0)1588 620489
www.bacheldremill.co.uk
Bacheldre Watermill, established in 1575, produces a range of organic and heritage flours using traditional equipment, some of which is hundreds of years old.

They sell organic stoneground flours including spelt, rye and a malted blend. Their products are available from stockists throughout the UK or online.

Doves Farm
Salisbury Road
Hungerford, Berkshire, RG17 0RF
+44 (0)1488 684880
www.dovesfarm.co.uk
Doves Farm was established in 1978 and mills many different and rare types of grain, including spelt, kamut and einkorn. Doves also mill wheat, barley, rye, oats and quinoa. They offer 13 types of organic flour, including heritage wheat types. Doves also supply 25-kg sacks of organic rye grain and organic high protein wheat grain, and sell both roller- and stone-ground flours. Available online or from supermarkets.

Gilchesters Organics
Gilchesters
Hawkwell
Northumberland NE18 0QL
+44 (0) 1661 886119
www.gilchesters.com
This mill is situated two miles north of Hadrian's Wall and is built on the site of a Roman fort. The owners grow heritage grains using organic methods and grind them using stones. Rye flour, wholemeal spelt flour and wholemeal wheat flour can be ordered online, but their website also gives details of stockists of their products around the UK.

Golspie Mill
Dunrobin, Golspie
Sutherland, KW10 6SF
+44 (0)1408 633278
www.golspiemill.co.uk
One of very few traditional water-powered mills remaining in production in Scotland, Golspie dates from 1863 but was fully

restored in 1992. Golspie sells strong wholemeal bread flour, plain flour and rye flour, as well as oatmeal, all organic. Order online directly from the mill or see website for UK stockists.

Planet Organic
www.planetorganic.com
This online organic food shop sells a wide range of organic heritage and rye flours from different millers across the UK, as well as organic baking ingredients, including instant and fresh yeast.

Real Foods
+44 (0)131 556 1772
www.realfoods.co.uk
This organic online retailer sells wheat grains in bulk, including whole oat groats, kamut grains, sprouting wheat grains, spelt grains and rye grains, as well as flours such as wholegrain organic stoneground kamut, spelt, buckwheat and brown teff. In addition, they supply organic vegan spelt flakes, instant organic baking yeast and organic molasses.

Sharpham Park
Street
Somerset BA16 9SA
www.sharphampark.com
+44 (0)1458 844080
Sharpham Park, a 300-acre historic park near Glastonbury, dates back to the Bronze Age. Archaeological excavations revealed that spelt had been grown in the area since the Bronze and Iron Ages. Spelt is growing at Sharpham Park again today, with organic white or wholegrain spelt flour and an organic spelt and rye blend available directly online or through UK stockists. Sharpham Park also sell organic pearled spelt and organic spelt grain, spelt leaven and sourdough

starter. Sharpham Park's current owner, Roger Saul, has written a book called **Spelt** (see page 293).

Shipton Mill Ltd
Long Newton
Tetbury, Gloucestershire, GL8 8RP
+44 (0)1666 505050
www.shipton-mill.com
Set in a beautiful Cotswold valley near Tetbury, the mill has been producing flour since the time of the Domesday Book. Today Shipton Mill offers a range of organic flours, including einkorn, emmer, khorasan, spelt, both light and dark rye flour, as well as malt and barley flour. They also sell organic chopped rye grains and cut malted rye grains. Shipton Mill also sell organic fresh and instant yeast. Their website also offers tips and techniques, recipes, ideas, hints and inspiration.

Wessex Mill
Mill Street
Wantage, OX12 9AB
+44 (0)1235 768991
www.wessexmill.co.uk
As well as selling online a very wide range of flours, Wessex Mill offers 150-ml pots of both rye and wheat starter. They also sell dark matt flour, wholemeal rye flour, light rye, and both wholemeal and white spelt flour. You can also order a dough scraper from them.

Whole Foods Market UK
www.wholefoodsmarket.com
Now expanding in the UK, Whole Foods Market is an international company selling organic flour in bulk, including amaranth, faro, spelt and teff, as well as rye berries. You can either click on 'Find a Store' on their website to locate a shop, or order online.

WEBSITES ABOUT BAKING

www.breadandcompanatico.com
Blog documenting bread-making experiments by an Italian scientist living in Sweden.

www.breadtopia.com
Forum and blog.

www.thefreshloaf.com
Internationally recognized bread website with Q&As on baking.

www.sourdough.com
Site for bakers from all over the world sharing a passion for great bread.

www.wildyeastblog.com
The yeastspotting column collects and showcases beautiful breads.

BREADMAKING COURSES

Cornfield Bakery
76 High Street
Wheatley
Oxfordshire OX33 1XP
+44 (0)1865 872682
www.cornfieldbakery.com
As well as producing and delivering artisan bread, including their signature Cornfield Sourdough, Cornfield Bakery offers one-day bread-making courses with no more than six participants and taught by a master baker. The course covers a variety of breads including sourdough, and each participant is given a pot of starter to take home with them.

The Sourdough School
Northampton
+44 (0)7813 308301
www.sourdough.co.uk
The School offers extensive five-day courses and small

tutorial groups on sourdough bread and fermentation, taught by sourdough specialist Vanessa Kimball and award-winning baker Emmanuel Hadjiandreou. The Sourdough Diploma Course aims to give an in-depth understanding of the principles of sourdough, flour, digestibility, gluten, shaping and wild cultures and fermentation. Their website is a comprehensive and authoritative resource.

The School of Artisan Food
www.schoolofartisanfood.org
Lower Motor Yard
Welbeck, Notts, S80 3LR
+44 (0)1909 532171
This not-for-profit organization, offers courses to help you improve your bread-baking skills or learn more about becoming an artisan baker. They offer an introductory course in artisan bread baking as well as an Advanced Diploma in baking. Other courses specifically concentrates on using rye and heritage grains.

UNUSUAL SITES FOR INTEREST

Bread Matters
Macbiehill Farmhouse
Lamancha, West Linton
Peeblesshire EH46 7AZ
+44 (0)1968 660449
www.breadmatters.com
Bread Matters was created by Andrew Whitley (see details of his books, opposite) and Veronica Burke to promote the social, economic, cultural and health benefits of making bread with grain grown and milled in the region using slow fermentation and human-scale production. As well as teaching authoritative courses on how to bake real bread, Andrew is developing an organic agro-forestry project to help build a local grain economy.

Veronica Burke is developing Bread Matters' not-for-profit work in social inclusion, food justice, health equality and community involvement.

Real Bread Campaign
www.realbreadcampaign.org
The Real Bread Campaign is part of the charity Sustain, which is the alliance for better food and farming. The Real Bread Campaign's aim is to find and share ways to make bread better for us, better for our communities and better for the planet. They are working to secure funding to help unlock the social, therapeutic and employment opportunities offered by making real bread by hand. The campaign believes this will help people facing social exclusion due to a range of factors that might put them at a disadvantage, including living with mental health issues or physical disabilities. You can sign up to join the campaign online at the address given above.

Soil Association
South Plaza
Marlborough Street
Bristol BS1 3NX
+44 (0)117 314 5000
www.soilassociation.org
Champions of organic practice, the Soil Association operates as a charity and as a not-for-profit business. Their aim is to build a world where people, animals and the planet can thrive. The Soil Association's green leaf symbol on the label certifies that the flour or grains you are buying are guaranteed to be organic.

The Traditional Cornmillers Guild
tcmg.org.uk
tradmillers@gmail.com
Perhaps more so than in any other country, since the 1980s, many British mills have been rescued, restored and, very often, brought back into full use. The Guild provides information, support for and advice about the increasing numbers of traditional windmills and watermills that have remained in production or have been brought back into full working order. Most of the Guild mills are open to visitors and offer tours and events and have tearooms and millshops. Visit the website for information about finding a mill in your area.

RECOMMENDED BOOKS

Richard Bertinet
Crust: From Sourdough, Spelt and Rye Bread to Ciabatta, Bagels and Brioche (2012)
Kyle Cathie, London

Richard Bertinet
Dough: Simple Contemporary Bread
Kyle Cathie, London (2016)

Emily Buehler
Bread Science: The Chemistry and Craft of Making Bread
Two Blue Books, Hillsborough (2006)

Joanne Chang
Flour: Spectacular Recipes from Boston's Flour Bakery + Café
Chronicle Books, San Francisco (2010)

Toy Kim Dupree
Amy's Bread, Revised and Updated: Artisan-style breads, sandwiches, pizzas, and more from New York City's favourite bakery
John Wiley & Sons, Inc., Hoboken (2010)

Ken Forkish
Flour Water Salt Yeast: The Fundamentals of Artisan Bread and Pizza
Ten Speed Press, Berkeley (2012)

Stanley Ginsberg
The Rye Baker: Classic Breads from Europe and America
W.W. Norton & Company, New York (2016)

Zachary Golper & Peter Kaminsky
Bien Cuit: The Art of Bread
Regan Arts., New York (2015)

Emmanuel Hadjiandreou
How to Make Sourdough: 45 Recipes for Great-tasting Sourdough Breads That are Good for you, too
Ryland, Peters & Small, London, (2016)

Jeffrey Hamelman
Bread: A Book of Techniques and Recipes
Wiley, New Jersey (2012)

Jeff Hertzberg M.D. and Zoë François
The New Artisan Bread in Five Minutes a Day: The Discovery that Revolutionizes Home Baking
Thomas Dunne Books, New York (2013)

Ciril Hitz
Baking Artisan Pastries & Breads: Sweet and Savory Baking for Breakfast, Brunch, and Beyond
Crestline, New York (2012)

Thomas Keller
The Bouchon Bakery (The Thomas Keller Library)
Workman Publishing Company Inc., New York (2012)

Jim Lahey
My Bread: The Revolutionary No-Work, No-Knead Method
W.W. Norton & Co., New York (2009)

Daniel Leader
Local Breads: Sourdough and Whole-grain Recipes From Europe's Best Artisan Bakers
W.W. Norton & Company, New York (2007)

Dan Lepard & Richard Whittington
Baking with Passion: Exceptional Recipes for Real Breads, Cakes and Pastries
Quadrille, London (2010)

Tess Lister
A Handful of Flour: Recipes from Shipton MIll
Heaadline, London (2016)

Sarah Owens
Sourdough: Recipes for Rustic Fermented Breads, Sweets, Savories, and More
Roost Books, Boston & London (2015)

Emilie Raffa
Artisan Sourdough Made Simple: A Beginner's Guide & Beyond to Delicious Handcrafted Bread with Minimal Kneading
Page Street Publishing, Salem (2017)

The Real Bread Campaign
Knead to Know: The Real Bread Starter: The Introductory Guide to Success in Baking for your Local Community
Grub Street, London (2013)

Peter Reinhart
The Bread Baker's Apprentice, 15th Anniversary Edition: Mastering the Art of Extraordinary Bread
Ten Speed Press, Berkeley (2016)

Peter Reinhart
Bread Revolution: World-Class Baking with Sprouted and Whole Grains, Heirloom Flours, and Fresh Techniques
Ten Speed Press, Berkeley (2014)

Peter Reinhart
Peter Reinhart's Whole Grain Breads: New Techniques, Extraordinary Flavour
Ten Speed Press, Berkeley (2007)

Chad Robertson
Tartine Bread
Chronicle Books, San Francisco (2010)

Chad Robertson
Tartine Book No.3: Modern Ancient Classic Whole
Chronicle Books, San Francisco (2013)

Roger Saul
Spelt: Cakes, Cookies, Breads & Meals
Watkins Media, London, (2015)

Michel Suas
Advanced Bread and Pastry
Delmar Cengage Learning, Clifton Park (2008)

Andrew Whitley
Bread Matters: How and Why to Make Your Own
Andrews McMeel, London, (2009)

Andrew Whitley
Do Sourdough: Slow Bread for Busy Lives
Do Book Company, London, (2014)

Chris Young and the Bakers of the Real Bread Campaign
Slow Dough: Real Bread: Baker's Secrets for Making Amazing Long-Rise Loaves at Home Bread for Busy Lives
Nourish Books, London, (2016)

INDEX

THANK YOU

A heartfelt thank you to Rhonda Crosson, Thomas Koch, Thomas Steinmann, and Martin Marko Hansen for their huge efforts as this book materialized. And an equally heartfelt thank you goes out to each and every person at our bakeries – and those in retail and wholesale – for their daily efforts. Tirelessly, you continue the fight to raise our bread culture to the next level.

MEYER'S BAKERY

An Hachette UK Company
www.hachette.co.uk

Originally published in Danish in 2014 by Lindhardt og Ringhof

First published in Great Britain in 2017 by Mitchell Beazley, a division of Octopus Publishing Group Ltd
Carmelite House
50 Victoria Embankment
London EC4Y 0DZ
www.octopusbooks.co.uk

ISBN 978 1 78472 354 5

Printed and bound in China

10 9 8 7 6 5 4 3 2 1

Text: Claus Meyer
Consultants: Thomas Steinmann, Thomas Koch, Martin Marko Hansen
Designer: Birgitte Tommerup
Photographer: Stine Christiansen/Skovdal Nordic (www.skovdalnordic.com)
Translator: Iben Philipsen
Editor (for UK and US): Constance Novis